SUPREMACY SRI
AKAL TAKHT SAHIB
DE JURE

JASDEV SINGH RAI

Opinion and Proposal Paper requested by
Last Sardar Gurcharan singh Tohra (President of SGPC for 27 years)

Opinion and Proposal Paper
Jasdev Singh Rai

PARTRIDGE

To order additional copies of this book, contact
Partridge India
000 800 919 0634 (Call Free)
+91 000 80091 90634 (Outside India)
orders.india@partridgepublishing.com

www.partridgepublishing.com/india

CONTENTS

SUMMARY OF CONTENTS

ISSUES

The section on issues briefly explains the history of Sri Akal Takht Sahib, the role the institution plays in the lives of Sikhs, the office of Jathedar Sri Akal Takht Sahib, the current limitations on scope of Sri Akal Takht Sahib due to political and legal intrusions and what would be an ideal status in international relations.

CONCEPTS

This section deals with three distinctive aspects of GurSikhi and the challenges Sikhs face in the current world. The first deals with the principles and dynamics of consensus in GurSikhi and as intended in the Sikh community. It explains the challenges this faces.

The second is the concept of non-duality, a worldview in which the spiritual and temporal are not separated nor is there a concept of religion and secular in GurSikhi. The chapter explains the composite and comprehensive worldview of GurSikhi and the limitations to its development in modern times.

The third part briefly explains the unique corporate identity and structure of Sikhs consistent with GurSikhi and diversity of interpretations within GurSikhi as well as unifying role of Sri Akal Takht Sahib.

OPTIONS

This section looks at the options available to Sikhs to develop their worldview, systems of governance, etc. It examines critically both benefits and complexities at the idea of a Sikh State, and autonomous region within South Asia, status quo and GurSikhi as religion or world view as well as non-territorial nation character of Sikh nation.

THE PROPOSAL

This section sets out in detail the proposal for a self-governing Statehood option for Sri Akal Takht Sahib, full or observer membership at UN and a way forward to have a supporting world organisation. It also looks at the possibility of extra territorial arrangement for Sri Akal Takht Sahib.

SUMMARY

This section very briefly summarises the book.

"The Sikhs need independent representation at the UN and to deal with Governments around the world as a people"

'PANTH RATTAN' SARDAR GURCHARAN SINGH TOHRA

DEDICATION

One afternoon in December 2003, I had a long meeting with the late Sardar Gurcharan Singh Tohra in Patiala. He was resting after another day of protests by the Akali Dal. Sardar Tohra was a complex personality with deep Panthic sympathies but engaged in realistic and pragmatic politics, which sometimes forced him to compromise his own aims and ethics. Much has been said in the public arena about him.

I had requested this meeting to discuss the implications of World Heritage Status for Sri Darbar Sahib, were it to be granted. After listening, he took immediate steps to help me to stop this process. He then raised issues from a previous discussion I had with him two years earlier in London at Giani Amolak Singh's house. He reminded me that it was about Sri Akal Takht Sahib gaining status at the United Nations, and the SGPC along with other Sikh organisations getting some form of representation at the UN. Sardar Tohra then asked me to write a strategy paper.

I prepared a four-page brief. Unfortunately, Sardar Tohra's health deteriorated rapidly and sadly he passed away before he could read the brief. However, that proposal has now been converted into this book explaining the rationale and proposed steps to achieve a position of international relations consistent with the status of Sri Akal Takht Sahib, as intended. This book has been expanded to include and explain the background rationale.

Jasdev Singh Rai

INTRODUCTION

Since 1920 when the Shiromani Gurdwara Parbhandik Committee, generally known as SGPC and the Akali Dal were formed, the Sikhs have been a formidable political force in contemporary India despite being small in numbers compared to the overall population of South Asia. Their political clout was immense during the decolonisation struggles. The sacrifices of the Sikhs and their eagerness to commit to peaceful struggles gave them an edge over many other communities.

Despite this political dividend, the Sikhs were lost. They lacked clear strategies and were strung along by high politics of the time. Survival as a distinct community became important. Through difficult and trying times the Akali Dal did its best. The division of human affairs into a dualism of secular and religious with the latter a matter in the personal domain imposed by western hegemony in the contemporary world played havoc with Sikhs. In an era of nation states, democratic rule and secular polity, the Sikhs have been determined to maintain their comprehensive non-dualist approach. The Indian civilisation has been a non-dualist world for most of its 5000 years until Nehru's passion for European secularism forced a new direction in Indian public life in 1947. Nehru and other secularists reacted to the divide and rule policies of British imperialism which had introduced communal tensions in the political class, by adopting a European solution despite the fact that India's own pluralistic civilisation had successfully absorbed distinct communities and dissipated communal tendencies through its history. Under the influence of European academics and Nehruvian elite, India abandoned 5000 years of Indian philosophical and political tradition in preference for European paradigm as its foundation which forms the basis of the current post 1947 Indian Constitution. The majority of Sikhs resisted this denial of Indic thought and insult to Indian civilisation in Indian public life by adamantly continuing with the Akali Dal as a political party in the public arena.

The transfer of power in 1947 from British Empire to a pan Indian political State and political class has meant that the central institutions of the Sikhs were not able to regain their independent status from British colonialism in real terms. As a result, the Sikh Panth cannot independently develop concepts and solutions to meet challenges of the period or sustain its essential beliefs. Subject to different jurisdictions in different countries, the Sikhs have had to make conscious and sometimes strategic compromises or adjustments of the distinctive features of their concepts that are at odds with the secular Nation-State. The Sikhs have been segregated into different bodies within States (countries) and have not developed a mechanism of collective international decision making and action. They are dependent on the goodwill of a few nation states to take up their international issues. These issues, when taken up, are often complicated by the prerogatives and politics of the State. The status of Sikhs and their current predicaments call for a review of the current situation and embark on sensible as well as pragmatic steps to come to terms with changed circumstances and resolve the complexities and tangles in which they have found themselves.

There is no doubt that the Sikhs as a people, or Global community, need to engage with governments around the world and with international institutions independently of States and other organisations. The Sikhs need to be able to research into issues and decide on strategies as well as solutions that are consistent with worldview and concepts of GurSikhi and that are made without constraints imposed by the politics and constitutions of the countries in which major Sikh organisations are situated. The two courses of direct interaction for Sikhs in the international sphere are firstly to have a representative body with an international NGO status with limited influence and secondly some form of full membership of the UN as a representative State member for the Global Sikh community. Both can be taken up concurrently and are detailed here.

The book first sets out the issue and a need for an independent centralised institution followed by a background discussion on the distinctive aspects of Sikh philosophy and concepts that need to breathe and exist in an independent sphere without the interests and politics of various parties. The third part examines the options available to Sikhs to create an independent space and the way forward. The book finally proposes a structured process to establishing supremacy of Sri Akal Takht Sahib in the international world. The book is neither an argument for or against a separate Sikh State nor is it attacking or endorsing the integrity of India. Both these matters are outside the scope of this book.

It is through this freedom of operations that Sikhs can best resolve the many issues that face the community and the challenges that GurSikhi has to endure in being a distinctive concept and worldview. It will also enable Sikhs to contribute to the world with constructive and innovative solutions to the world's many problems.

Jasdev Singh Rai

ISSUES

SRI AKAL TAKHT SAHIB

JATHEDAR SRI AKAL TAKHT SAHIB

FUNCTIONAL RELEVANCE OF SRI AKAL TAKHT SAHIB

SOCIAL ISSUES

COLLECTIVE DECISIONS

UNIQUE CONCEPTS

REGIONAL OR INTERNATIONAL

RESTRICTIONS AND LIMITATIONS

STATUS QUO

INDIAN CONSTITUTION AND GURDWARA ACT

AKALI DAL

THE CASE FOR SRI AKAL TAKHT SAHIB TO BE INDEPENDENT OF
ANY LEGAL OR POLITICAL SHADOW

SRI AKAL TAKHT SAHIB

Constructed in 1608, Sri Akal Takht Sahib is literally translated as the throne of the 'Immortal'. It was built by the sixth Guru, Guru Hargobind Sahib Ji. The original design was a platform. According to historical narrative, the Guru used to sit on it and discharge decisions, arbitrate in disputes, clarify matters and give orders. The platform was considered a throne. The Mughal Emperors were not tolerant of this new institutional development of Sikhs.

Sri Akal Takht Sahib is in the precincts of Sri Darbar Sahib. It is opposite the main building, Sri Harmandir Sahib. Sri Harmandir Sahib is surrounded by a pool of water with a causeway to get to land. There is a large entrance doorway to this causeway called Darshan Deori. Sri Harmandir Sahib is built to be slightly lower than the surrounding ground to express humility and that the 'Eternal' is also among the lowest of the low in society. Its physically lowered position also expresses a profound concept in GurSikhi, that everything evolves from the same base. In GurSikhi, the eternal reality is a oneness of all that is manifest and is unmanifest (Naadh-Anadh). It is not about power over everything. The oneness is the most powerful and the least powerful as manifestation of the same. Hence Sri Harmandir Sahib does not attempt to express power but a connection from the most basic, a sublimity and an inter connectedness.

Sri Akal Takht Sahib on the other hand is now on a slightly raised ground reflecting its position as a place of temporal authority of the Sikhs. The architecture is such that Sri Harmandir Sahib cannot be seen from Sri Akal Takht Sahib but the Takht can be seen from Sri Harmandir Sahib. The significance of this is that while Sri Harmandir Sahib is of cosmological significance where Sri Guru Granth Sahib is recited every day through Kirtan and 'Paath' (saying or chanting without instruments), Sri Akal Takht Sahib is of temporal significance where decisions, arbitrations and edicts are made for Sikhs and it functions as an institution representing Sikhs. Sri Darbar Sahib is in Amritsar.

The Sri Akal Takht has had a complex history. It was initially called Akal Bunga. After Guru Hargobind Sahib, the Gurus who followed the sixth Guru did not sit on the Takht. It became a central place of Sikhs after the 10th Guru, Guru Gobind Singh ji and became the place where Sikhs gathered to make collective decisions of all sorts including mediation. It became a place where Sikhs were gathering twice a year during the Misl period which was most of the later part of eighteenth century. Misls were large groups of Sikh warriors under a chief (or warlord). There were eleven Misls that often worked together against common enemies. The gathering at Sri Akal Takht Sahib was called 'Sarbat Khalsa' meaning Khalsa from around the world. The Takht began to acquire the status of the Sikh throne after Guru Gobind Singh ji.

Maharaja Ranjit Singh brought an end to the institution of Sarbat Khalsa as he felt threatened by it as a parallel authority. However, he did not take on the head of Sri Akal Takht Sahib, called Jathedar, because the latter was also 'Jathedar' or leader of one of the Misls with a significant force. But without the Sarbat Khalsa Sri Akal Takht Sahib's scope to establish a Sikh polity independent of the State was limited.

The British subsequently ensured that not only did the Sarbat Khalsa not take place but that the institution of Sri Akal Takht Sahib did not act independently. They appointed the custodian of Sri Akal Takht Sahib. The official title was Sabrah. Finally, in November 1920 a Sarbat Khalsa did take place after an incident where the British interfered directly in the affairs of the Takht and Sri Darbar Sahib. The Sarbat Khalsa unanimously chose a 'Jathedar' of Sri Akal Takht Sahib. The title has become the official title of the occupant at the seat of Sri Akal Takht Sahib.

Currently the legal status of Sri Akal Takhat Sahib is indeterminate. Officially it is not registered as an institution anywhere. The Indian State treats it as a defacto supremacy, but inherited a number of legal arrangements and instruments from the Colonial power that effectively enables the State to 'control' the Sri Akal Takht Sahib. While Sri Akal Takht is considered Supreme or as seat of Sikh sovereignty by Sikhs and treated as such by India and other as de facto, it does not have de jure Supremacy or Sovereignty in international relations.

JATHEDAR SRI AKAL TAKHT SAHIB

Every institution has a management system in place and so does Sri Akal Takht Sahib. While it is Sri Akal Takht Sahib that is the symbolic and significant central and authoritative institution of the Sikhs worldwide, the institution's management is under a custodian and a 'leader' now titled Jathedar Singh Sahib Sri Akal Takht Sahib.

The Jathedar is the ultimate spokesperson, head of consensus and arbiter of the world-wide Sikh community, acting through the office or the institution of Sri Akal Takht Sahib. The Jathedar is not a religious pontiff nor an infallible head within Sikhdom. The Jathedar brings consensus, manages consensus of opinions, ambitions, etc., and announces a decision after consensus. There are five Takhts in Sikhdom

- **Takht Sri Akal Takht Sahib at Sri Darbar Sahib, Amritsar**
- **Takht Sri Kesgarh Sahib, Anandpur Sahib, Punjab**
- **Takht Sri Patna Sahib, Patna, Bihar**
- **Takht Sach Khand Sri Hazur Sahib, Nanded, Maharasthra**
- **Takht Sri DamDama Sahib, Talwandi Sabo, Punjab**

Sri Akal Takht Sahib is the first of the Takhts and as it was established by the sixth Guru himself, it is considered as the focal and supreme Takht where all come to make final consensus decisions and from where decisions are announced.

On most issues there are five Jathedars from the Five Takhts of the Sikhs who come together to develop consensus. The Jathedar of Sri Akal Takht Sahib is the leader among the Jathedars and announces the decisions reached by consensus. Where there are no controversies or differences, the Jathedar Sri Akal Takht will clarify, release statements or make announcements without consulting the other four.

The Jathedar was not always called Jathedar. During Colonial rule, the custodian of this seat was called Sabrah.

The Jathedar was chosen just for the particular Sarbat Khalsa. However, the office became institutionalised to some extent during the Misl period and particularly during Maharajah Ranjit Singh's Kingdom.

Ideally the Jathedar is selected by Sikhs among themselves in a Sarbat Khalsa as explained later. In the last three decades the SGPC has been appointing Jathedars. In the absence of a Sarbat Khalsa, the appointed Jathedar has been often called 'acting Jathedar'.

FUNCTIONAL RELEVANCE OF SRI AKAL TAKHT SAHIB

Sri Akal Takht is of great importance and tremendous relevance to Sikhs and GurSikhi. Three essential functions that can be identified among others are:

1) The institution where guidance on Sikh codes of conduct, social ethics and living is provided, where thinkers and spiritually enlightened Sikhs gather to formulate interpretations of Sri Guru Granth Sahib by consensus and where different practices are standardised.

2) It serves as a centralising institution where collective decisions are made by consensus on the status of Sikhs, strategies of coordination, political survival of the community and on interpretations.

3) Where GurSikhi is given the opportunity to evolve its own unique worldview without restrictions and be able to strengthen ethical and social perspectives within Sikhs and contribute ideas to a changing world.

All these are carried out through the unique form of consensus forming in Sikhs called Sarb Samati, that means near unanimous decision making.

SOCIAL ISSUES

One of the main roles of Sri Akal Takht Sahib is to interpret GurSikhi into social issues and social practices of the Sikhs. It is here where general guidance to Sikhs on matters such as marriage, divorce, treatment of weaker members of society, attitudes toward sharing, poverty, modern education, euthanasia, etc, have to be discussed and finally decided for the community. Currently the Sikhs rely on a 1930s initiated and finally approved by SGPC in 1945 document titled 'Rehat Maryada'. Some prominent Sikh institutions do not accept this as authoritative since it was not decided at Sri Akal Takht Sahib and moreover view it as a document influenced by a statutory body of the State. This contention remains till today. It has led to significant schisms and sometimes conflict among various groups and schools of thought. It has to be resolved at a Sarbat Khalsa.

COLLECTIVE DECISIONS

Sri Akal Takht Sahib serves as a centralising institution where collective decisions are made by consensus on the status of Sikhs, strategies of coordination, political co-existence of the community with rest of the world and on interpretations.

Sri Akal Takht Sahib provides the common platform where Sikhs come together as a global community to decide and get guidance on every day political and related issues. As the institution of relevance to all Sikhs, ideally it should coordinate a common strategic approach across the world for Sikhs. For instance, if the Sikh community is facing discrimination in a part of the world, an effective administrative system at Sri Akal Takht Sahib could assist the community by advising the community how Sikhs handled a similar issue elsewhere. It could request Sikhs from another part of the world to advise and negotiate on their behalf with the relevant government. Sri Akal Takht Sahib could ideally encourage Sikhs across the world to assist each other in setting up schools, social enterprises, encourage Sikhs to engage in political representation, etc. It is at Sri Akal Takht Sahib that interpretations into practical engagements with the world, as Sikhs, have been decided in history most successfully.

UNIQUE CONCEPTS

Sri Akal Takht Sahib is the penultimate place where GurSikhi is given the opportunity to evolve its own unique worldview without restrictions and be able to strengthen ethical and social perspectives within Sikhs and contribute ideas to a changing world.

The Sikhs do have some unique concepts on many issues, such as environment, political governance, development, distribution of resources, etc. Many of these are being explored in various academic institutions around the world by Sikhs without any sense of coherence among them. Part of the disparate approaches and interpretations is that they are considerably influenced or sanctioned by the jurisdictions in which they are located. Ideally it is the Sri Akal Takht Sahib that could bring the greatest minds together and ensure that their work is consistent with GurSikhi, able to bring the enlightened minds and the scholars on a platform and promote unique and original perspectives that can be sourced in the Sri Guru Granth Sahib and the teachings of the Gurus.

REGIONAL OR INTERNATIONAL

The relevance of Sri Akal Takht Sahib is beyond Amritsar, beyond Punjab and in fact even beyond India. It is a global institution of the Sikhs. Decisions, interpretations and guidance from Sri Akal Takht Sahib influence every Sikh and his/her status in the Sikh community. For instance, Amritdhari Sikhs as opposed to Sikhs with unshorn hair are considered to have complete commitment to GurSikhi, hence qualified to hold positions within Gurdwaras according to statements from Sri Akal Takht Sahib. Within Amritdharis, certain schools of thought are considered to be closer to Sri Akal Takht Sahib than others.

Although quite a few disparate movements have emerged within Sikhs, possibly due to the centre being weakened, there is still among Sikhs a sense that the ultimate authority of interpretation and guidance on GurSikhi, Sikh ethics and practices is Sri Akal Takht Sahib. While some disregard the authority of the Jathedar for the time being because the Jathedar is considered to be a political appointee, they still hope that there will be a restoration of the seat of Jathedar free from the politics of the State. Others continue to hold decisions of the Jathedar in reverence and blame themselves for allowing the position of the Jathedar to have been politicised. Overall, Sikhs agree that Sri Akal Takht Sahib has a global relevance in the lives of the Sikhs.

The SGPC on the other hand is seen as a local body of the Sikhs in Punjab since the remit of Gurdwara Act has been limited to Punjab. The SGPC is a body of 'elected' individuals, elected on a British Westminster system of first past the post and theoretically working with a majority mandate. Sri Akal Takht Sahib on the other hand is not an institution working selectively for one majority view, group or political mandate. Nor is it a local, national or regional institution. Its remit is worldwide, in the Global Sikh community.

RESTRICTIONS AND LIMITATIONS

Through history, Sri Akal Takht Sahib has been an inspiration to the Sikhs. Here they have gathered as a People, here they decided and from here they advanced as a united People although with some dissenting groups. It was always as a free and proud people. Yet when Sri Akal Takht Sahib was under the jurisdiction of another power, the Sikhs generally descended into fractious and self-absorbed people.

Currently the people who appoint the Jathedar and influence his function, pay for the office and staff, are elected by Indian citizens in one state, the Punjab. These citizens are Sikhs. They are elected by a simple majoritarian election onto the body called SGPC. They have to be Amritdhari Sikhs. To be successful, candidates have to spend considerable money to persuade Sikh voters in their constituency in Punjab to vote for them. Like all simple majority elections, the aspirants are critical of the candidates standing against them. Often, they are also derogatory of opposition candidates.

Candidates for the elections in SGPC often spend considerable amount of money in winning over voters. Usually they belong to a political party or are backed by one. The successful candidate is indebted to the political party and its leader and generally follows the orders of the political party.

As SGPC has assumed the authority to appoint the 'Jathedar', this means the SGPC members will appoint the person who their political party directs them to put forward. The freedom of the office of the Jathedar is compromised by this process. The Office cannot operate freely to represent the Global Sikh community. The political party also tries to restrict the office of Jathedar from engaging independently with politicians opposed to the leader of the party that controls SGPC. It therefore restricts the scope of the Jathedar to bring the community together in consensus.

Secondly the Jathedar has to be an Indian citizen in the current legal situation. There is no scope within the Indian legal system for a non-citizen to be 'elected' or 'selected' to any office of an Indian institution. Although Sri Akal Takht Sahib is not a registered institution in India, nevertheless it is treated as an Indian institution. Moreover, as the SGPC appoints the Jathedar, it assumes that the person has to be an Indian citizen. A non-citizen will have to acquire special residence status and a work permit. The Sikhs cannot appoint the person best suited for the office from the world-wide community even if the Akali Dal were to be magnanimous and draw back from interfering in the selection of the Jathedar.

As an Indian citizen, the Jathedar is subject to the freedoms and restrictions of the Indian Constitution and the prerogatives of the Indian State. This also means obeying the laws of India, respecting its international treaties, respecting its engagements in international affairs and upholding its territorial integrity. The Jathedar is therefore not independent or able to represent the worldwide Sikh community without permission from the Indian State. Nor can the Jathedar engage in any discussion that is considered 'anti national' by the Indian State. For instance, the scope of the Jathedar to be representative of Sikhs of Pakistan or many Sikhs in Canada is considerably restricted.

Further, the Office of the Jathedar is dependent on the financial and administrative support from the SGPC. The office cannot receive funds directly from abroad nor can it appoint non-Indian citizens to work in the office as specialists. Any decisions taken by the office of the Jathedar can potentially be challenged in Indian courts, although so far this has been avoided.

The Indian State can restrict the activities of the Office of the Jathedar, ensure that they do not foray into politics or what the State might conceive as political ideas inimical to its perspectives on political theory or prerogatives. If Sikhs in another country face issues concerned with following their practices and might need intervention or advice from Sri Akal Takht Sahib, there are potential problems as the Jathedar cannot engage with foreign governments directly. If that group of Sikhs has been vocal against the Sikh political party in control of SGPC, the Jathedar can be persuaded to resist giving any assistance. Moreover, if the Indian State has tensions or poor relations with that country, the ability of Sri Akal Takht Sahib to offer assistance could be limited.

The Indian State, like most States would prefer the Office of the Jathedar to concentrate on religion as worshippers and simply delve on matters to do with 'God' rather than social theory, political ideas, society, etc. However, even within this limited and restricted scope for GurSikhi, in practice, there are problems. In the last decade there have been a few instances where the Jathedar has taken an interpretational position against another eminent Sikh or scholar, whether within India or in another country, based not on an independent and well-argued position, but by siding with the organisation that has the most influence within SGPC.

It is obvious that from the restrictions the Office of Jathedar faces, they do affect and will affect the very notion of supremacy of the Sri Akal Takht Sahib. Sri Akal Takht Sahib may be treated as a de facto independent institution by successive Governments of India, but legally and politically it can neither function independently nor really act as the institution to guide the Global Sikh community, impartially, independently and consistent with guidance from Sri Guru Granth Sahib.

STATUS QUO

Currently Sri Akal Takht Sahib has no legal status of any sort either in India or internationally. The Sarbat Khalsa of 1920 selected a Jathedar to replace the British backed Sabrah. At the same time an organisation was established to manage the historically instituted Sikh Gurdwaras and the main Sikh institutions and shrines. This was called the Shiromani Gurdwara Parbhandik Committee or SGPC for short.

The SGPC was given the responsibility by the Sikhs to manage the process of selecting a Jathedar from the Sikhs and to provide the infrastructure assistance to manage the affairs of Sri Akal Takht Sahib. Essentially this was done as the SGPC was the largest and most organised institutional body and Sri Akal Takht Sahib did not have its own set up, having been restricted from doing so during British colonial rule. The SGPC was not given 'authority' to appoint the Jathedar. This difference has often not been appreciated by Sikhs and non-Sikhs. The SGPC was handed the responsibility to organise and manage the appointment of the Jathedar but not the 'authority' to appoint the Jathedar. The SGPC carried out its responsibility by organising consensus among the various schools of thought, seminaries and large Sikh institutions. When a proposed individual was acceptable to all, SGPC arranged the ceremony. All the participant institutions and seminaries gave formal acceptance. Since the privilege to manage the appointment was given by the Sarbat Khalsa to the SGPC, the Sarbat Khalsa can also take back that responsibility at any time.

In 1925, after sustained struggle by Sikhs, the British colonial power started to hand over management of Sikh shrines to the SGPC by enacting the Gurdwara Act 1925. The Act was to empower a Sikh elected body to manage Sikh shrines and Gurdwaras. The body was officially called the 'Board'. This included managing Sri Harmandir Sahib and almost everything in Sri Darbar Sahib complex, except the institution of Sri Akal Takht Sahib. Within Sri Akal Takht Sahib complex, there is a Gurdwara as well with its own Granthis, one of whom is a Head Granthi. The Act empowered the body (the Board) to appoint the Head Granthi of the Gurdwara in Sri Akal Takht Sahib and manage the Gurdwara.

The Gurdwara Act formally recognised the Shiromani Gurdwara Parbhandik Committee as the 'Board'. SGPC, first introduced as a common organisation of the Sikhs for managing Gurdwaras in 1920, became a statutory body after 1925. A statutory body is a State body bound by the limits and provisions of the Constitution of the country.

The appointment or selection of Jathedar was not included in the Act. Neither was the institution, Sri Akal Takht Sahib, the seat of Miri-Piri, that is spiritual and temporal, among Sikhs, mentioned in the Act. The Gurdwara in Sri Akal Takht Sahib is mentioned. The reason may be quite simple. The Act is a State Act which was enacted to set up a statutory body with legal rights and authority to manage Sikh Shrines. As such, it is directly under the State. However, the State does not have the privilege to interpret, adjudicate between religious schools

12

or influence codes of personal conduct in a religion. For instance, the State cannot direct the Catholic Church that women priests must be ordained, nor can it insist that Muslims only pray on Friday during day time and not in the rest of the week, nor can it tell Hindus that they should stop worshipping Kali, etc. Similarly, the State cannot set up a committee, a management Board or a judicial committee to tell Sikhs whether to recite the five Bani's (prayers) or seven Bani's when taking Amrit (initiation into order of Khalsa) or whether Raag Malla should be read or not. These are issues of interpretation, practices and religious codes beyond the scope of a secular State. The State can manage the secular aspects of a religious institution, such as running of services as decided by the religious authorities, disbursement of funds, service contracts, security and so on. The role of the Jathedar is interpretation, building consensus on religious and spiritual issues among others and arbitrate on these matters as well as to lay, by consensus, the practices etc of the Sikhs and to ensure Sikhs and Sikh institutions are compliant with GurSikhi, its ethos and its accepted practices. These are activities that are outside the jurisdiction of the State, especially in a secular State. Hence the Gurdwara Act remained outside this area and outside the institution of Sri Akal Takht Sahib. The Gurdwara Act remains within the remit of the Indian Constitution.

INDIAN CONSTITUTION AND THE GURDWARA ACT

The Constitution of India clearly states that:

Article 25. Freedom of conscience and free profession, practice and propagation of religion.

(2) Nothing in this article shall affect the operation of any existing law or prevent the State from making any law—

(*a*) regulating or restricting any economic, financial, political or other secular activity which may be associated with religious practice.

Thus Article 25.2.a states the areas in which the State is entitled to interfere in a religion. It is 'regulating or restricting any economic, financial, political or other secular activity'. The Constitution does not permit the State to decide on interpretation, tinker with the Rehat Maryada (codes of conduct), practices and rituals, etc, of a religion that are not of secular nature.

Since the SGPC is the Board in the Gurdwara Act 1925, it cannot take responsibility for or interfere in anything within Sikh institutions other than secular issues such as administration or management. Hence it is called Management committee. Its powers are no more than those of the Gurdwara Committee of any Gurdwara around the world.

The Gurdwara Act starts with the preamble:

'An Act to provide for the better administration of certain Sikh Gurdwaras and the inquiries into matter connected therewith.'

The Act does not say to interpret, adjudicate between schools of thought, or set codes of conduct, etc, or to act as the representative body of Sikh religion. The act limits its scope to that consistent with the Constitution and therefore imposes those limits upon the SGPC as well.

In the definitions, the Act defines office in 4. (i) as

4) (i) "Office" means any office by virtue of which the holder thereof participates in the management or performance of public worship in a Gurdwara or in the management or performance of any rituals or ceremonies observed therein and "office-holder" means any person who holds an office.

The institution of Sri Akal Takht Sahib is not a place for the 'worship or management of performance of rituals or ceremonies' but a place where interpretations are decided. Once the interpretations, practices and codes of conduct are decided or adjudicated in a case of confusions, it is then up to the management to ensure that they are observed or instituted in practice in their Gurdwaras. Therefore the 'Office' according to the Gurdwara Act can get involved in the later but not in the former.

The Act gives power to a tribunal to define what is and is not a Gurdwara but in its Article 16.2. (i) it indicates what constitutes a Gurdwara:

'A Gurdwara was established by, or in memory of any of the Ten Sikh Gurus, or in commemoration of any incident in the life of any of the Ten Sikh Gurus and

1[was] used for public worship by Sikhs'.

Thus a Gurdwara is a place for worship. Sri Akal Takht Sahib is not a 'throne' for worshipping, but a 'throne' for deciding interpretations. Throughout the Act, the wording worship is used, thus differentiating Gurdwaras from Takhts. There is a Gurdwara in the building of Sri Akal Takht Sahib. It is the Head Granthi of this Gurdwara who officiates the ceremony of Sri Guru Granth Sahib leaving for Sri Harmandir Sahib (for Parkash) every morning and receiving for rest every evening (Sukhasan). The Head Granthi is officially appointed by SGPC for officiating ceremonies and is part of the Board of SGPC.

The Act mentions who can be in the Board, that is the SGPC, in Article 44 and 45 of the Gurdwara Act 1925.

44. (vi) and 45. 1.(iv) the head minister of the Darbar Sahib, Amritsar, or of one of the [five] Sikh Takhts

The word head minister has often mistakenly been interpreted as Jathedar. However, a 'minister' is also defined in the Act Article 4 (vii) as:

(vii) "Minister" means an office-holder to whom either solely or along with others the control of the management or performance of public worship in a gurdwara and of the rituals and ceremonies, observed therein is entrusted: Provided that an office-holder to whom either solely or along with others the performance of public worship in the Gurdwara and of the rituals and ceremonies observed therein is not entrusted directly shall not be deemed to be a Minister for the purpose of sections 134 and 135

A 'Minister' therefore is a 'Granthi', whose primary role is to conduct services or perform public worship. The primary role of the Jathedar is not as a Granthi but as the 'leader' of the Sikhs in interpretations, etc.

All the Takhts, especially Sri Akal Takht Sahib do have a Gurdwara within them and have 'Head Granthis' or 'Head Ministers'. The Head Granthis are different than the Jathedars. The Act refers to them as Ministers and not Jathedars.

The Act also defines the role of SGPC in the Takhts, limiting it to secular issues. In Article 85, the Act states:

85.3.(1) The Board shall be the Committee of Management for the Gurdwaras known as- (i) The Sri Akal Takhat Sahib at Amritsar and Sri Takhat Kesgarh Sahib, Anandpur.

Here the SGPC can manage the administration of the Gurdwaras within the Takhts, but it cannot be running the primary purpose of the Takht, that of interpretation and adjudication.

In defining the role of the SGPC in any Gurdwara, Article 133 of the Act states: Subject to the provisions of this Act, a committee shall have full powers of control........to ensure the proper management of the Gurdwara or Gurdwaras and the efficient administration of the property, income and endowments thereof.

Hence neither the Constitution of India nor the Gurdwara Act empowers the SGPC to 'control' Sri Akal Takht Sahib or appoint or dismiss the Jathedar. That it has been doing so is more the weakness of the Sikhs. As a statutory body, the SGPC has also been acting in violation of the constitution of India by interfering in the interpretation and adjudication of Sikh religion by appointing the Jathedar.

The role of SGPC and that of Jathedar in deciding on interpretation and authorisation of practices became somewhat overlapped, perhaps more from misunderstanding and opportunism rather than intention. Strictly from a legal position, once the SGPC became the 'Board' empowered by the Act as a statutory body of the State, it cannot have authority or power to select or appoint or interfere in the affairs of the institution of Jathedar or Sri Akal Takht Sahib as detailed above. However, as the largest body of the Sikhs, it was given the privilege by the Sikh community to assist in organising the selection and appointment of the Jathedar and provide logistical support. This difference has often remained blurred. If the SGPC, acting as the Board, assumes authority to appoint the Jathedar, it will be violating the secular limitations of the State as detailed in the Indian Constitution. Hence it will be acting extra judicially.

Unfortunately, over the years, especially after 1984, the SGPC has been acting as the body with sole authority to 'appoint' the Jathedar, dismiss the Jathedar and even pontificate on interpretations. This activity has no basis in law or the Constitution. The SGPC cannot assume and assert sole authority as it is both illegal and unconstitutional. Moreover, the SGPC, as a State body, is under the control of State powers. The Indian State influences it indirectly by timing the election of its officers to coincide with its own security and other political interests. Any SGPC decision has also to be ratified by the District Commissioner, a civil servant of the Government. This therefore hands the power of appointment of Jathedar to the Government indirectly. This places the institution of Sri Akal Takht Sahib under the direct control of the State of India, although it is only the Gurdwara in Sri Akal Takht Sahib that is permitted by the Constitution to be under the Government of India.

The only redeeming aspect of the current actions of SGPC in appointing the Jathedar is that it officially gives the title 'Acting Jathedar'. This is an indication and admission that the substantive appointment of the Jathedar is not in its remit.

AKALI DAL

Another organisation set up in the 1920s was the Shiromani Akali Dal, a political body to represent the Sikhs in the communalised politics of south Asia in the run up to decolonisation. The Akali Dal was supposed to be guided in policy and its representational interests by the SGPC. Communal politics became even more stratified after 1947 as British India became divided into India and Pakistan after the end of colonialism. The Akali Dal continued to defend the interests of the Sikhs and came into power in Punjab. Having acquired State power and access to political largesse, the Akali Dal became the more powerful of the two bodies, thus reversing the roles with SGPC. For nearly 40 years it is the Akali Dal that has been deciding who gets into SGPC, what SGPC's priorities are and who SGPC appoints as Jathedar. This became blatant after 1984 when the attack on Sri Darbar Sahib by Indian authorities also led to the collapse of the checks and balances among Sikh institutions to ensure no one person or one institution became tyrannical.

Currently the Jathedar has effectively been an appointee of the political head of the Akali Dal. The president of Akali Dal's main concern is to ensure that the Jathedar does not attempt to undermine his (leader of Akali Dal's) power. Consequently, it is not the most able or representative Sikh selected by Sikhs, but the safest pair of hands appointed by the leader of Akali Dal, a state of affairs that undermines the very independent institution of Sri Akal Takht Sahib. The irony as described above, is that the very appointment of the Jathedar by SGPC is an unconstitutional and illegal act as it is a statutory body.

THE CASE FOR SRI AKAL TAKHT SAHIB TO BE INDEPENDENT OF ANY LEGAL OR POLITICAL SHADOW

There are arguments that what was necessary in the seventeenth century may not be relevant today. Some argue that in the days of the internet, the necessity of a physical centre is obsolete. Others put forward counter ideas of what 'Sikhism' is and that there is no such institution as a central authority among Sikhs.

These arguments seem to ignore the understanding of the value of historic institutions and their perpetuity in the survival, cohesion as well as core characteristic of any community, nation, religion, belief system, etc. Similarly, they fail to appreciate both the nature of Sri Akal Takht Sahib and the state of the current world. If one was to subscribe to the view that what was necessary in the seventeenth century may not be relevant today, then surely all institutions with long historic continuity, such as the Vatican, Mecca, Church of England, the British Monarchy etc can be made redundant. In fact, if there was ever a time for the need for a central institution of the Sikhs free from interference from legal or political authority, it is from the twentieth century onwards.

As Sikhs disperse across the globe, it is even more important for them to be able to engage with a central institution to seek guidance on very complex issues that face Sikhs in different parts of the world. Apart from the issues of identity, maintaining practices and ethics, there are many other aspects such as the accepted interpretation, the need to gain strength from each other, the need to learn from each other. Otherwise, without a hub, or interactive central institution there will be as many interpretations as Sikhs and as many schisms as Sikh groups. There is already a tendency in many regions of the world for Sikhs to be creating indigenised versions of GurSikhi with local customs and religious influences or influenced by trends within different States, that are often contrary to the teachings of the Gurus. There are also academics trying to interpret GurSikhi within western humanist frameworks, eroding or even distorting its intrinsic originality. Different academics are postulating different interpretations depending on compulsions of the academic institution, department, State or financial grant, etc. There is a need for a central institution where consensus can be built and guidance can be sought. Small deviations from an agreed set of practices and norms are not a problem. The real threat arises when the fundamentals of the teachings are distorted by lack of training, guidance and consorting with other traditions thus creating an unrecognisable hybrid ideology or sect.

Secondly, Sikhs have faced considerable problems around the world in maintaining their practices. Different jurisdictions around the world pose different challenges to the Sikhs. Some are sympathetic to religious practices, while others are hostile or simply lack an awareness or understanding of Sikh practices. Often Sikhs have to try and explain in the best way they can but lack the diplomatic and legal know how of different legal systems or do not have the political contacts to influence sympathetic accommodation of practices. Sikhs have either tried to appeal to the countries they live in to intervene or suffer the difficulties. A central institution that can develop expertise and diplomatic ties can be better disposed to coordinate and represent Sikhs in different countries with the relevant governments.

Thirdly, Sri Akal Takht Sahib was established as the supreme institution of the Sikhs with no legal or political authority to reign over it. In other words, it is an institution outside the sovereign jurisdiction of any other temporal power. Difficult as it was even during the period of the Mughal Empire, it has become almost impossible in the contemporary world when every inch of land on earth is under some country or other's sovereign reach. The law of a State applies to every institution within its jurisdiction. This means that there is no place on this earth where Sikhs can freely determine their decisions without reference to the law of the land they are in.

Currently in India, Sri Akal Takht Sahib has an interesting but complex status. It is not registered as a body under any legal category. It enjoys de facto supremacy among Sikhs and the Indian State attempts not to interfere in it directly. Yet the institution is managed and controlled by a statutory body of the State even if it is a body of Sikhs. Moreover, the State did attack it in 1984 in an attempt to undermine it and control it in a move which it called removing 'terrorists' from the building. The attack led to an immediate call for a separate Sikh state to protect Sri Akal Takht Sahib. However even in a Sikh State, the Takht could still be under the shadow of political rulers as it became under the influence of Akali Dal politicians after 1984.

As a place where consensus is formed around essential Sikh ethics, interpretations, engagement with different jurisdictional requirements and as an institution that can give guidance to Sikhs in different countries, offer diplomatic expertise as well as coordinate outcomes for the Sikhs across the world, Sri Akal Takht Sahib can do that effectively, freely, without interference from any political interests if it establishes a status independent of any jurisdiction, political power and further has a direct status as member at the United Nations where it can develop its diplomatic expertise.

CONCEPTS
APPLIED GURSIKHI

INTRODUCTION TO CONCEPTS

CONSENSUS
- **DECISION MAKING AND ACCOUNTABILITY AT SRI AKAL TAKHT SAHIB**
- **SARBAT KHALSA**
- **CURRENT CONSENSUS FORMATION IN SIKH INSTITUTIONS**
- **FORMS OF CONSENSUS**
- **SARB SAMTI A SIKH FORM OF CONSENSUS**

PHILOSOPHY, WESTERN DUALISM AND GURSIKHI
- **CONCEPTS FOR OUR TIMES**

CAN GURSIKHI SURVIVE AND THRIVE UNDER SECULARISM?
- **GENESIS OF MODERN SECULARISM**
- **THE LIMITING EFEFCT OF SECULAR ON GURSIKHI**
- **THE SCOPE OF GURSIKHI UNDER INDIAN SECULARISM**
- **RESISTANCE TO SECULARISATION AND ASSIMILATION**

INTRODUCTION TO CONCEPTS

A Sri Akal Takht that is independent of any external jurisdiction, will be of value to Sikhs as a central institution in the Sikh corporate identity and function. It can be a powerful guiding body for Sikhs in their personal life and their engagement with the world. However, it can also be an exciting source of new ideas, concepts and solutions to the world's issues, such as conflicts, poverty, inequalities, environment, etc.

In this section an argument is put forward on why an independent place is needed for Sikhs to search for, discuss and develop ideas, policies, proposals and concepts that are based on GurSikhi. Some of these can be the solutions that the world is seeking. This section explains some of the unique concepts that have been difficult to be scholarly developed because of the lack of a free space unconstrained by national, legal and political jurisdictions.

Gursikhi has some unique concepts on many aspects of human life, human governance and human development as well as metaphysics. Having unique concepts is only of value if they are better than the ones that already exist in the world or offer improvement. Otherwise, developing and instituting concepts with a label 'from Sikh thought' is merely engaging in identity politics, nationalism asserting a difference for the sake of being different even if it changes nothing for the average human being.

It is important to ask whether concepts from GurSikhi offer anything new. A more important question is whether the current systems of liberal ideology, secular democracy, human rights and rule of law are adequate. If there are no real problems, then perhaps there is no need to introduce a whole new way of conceptualising human governance and relations or even reality. If a Sikh worldview and ideas change very little or are not significantly different, then it might be an expensive and pointless industry simply to have a series of theoretical proposals with little useful impact. These are vital aspects that need to be addressed.

It is important to consider the current paradigms in which the world operates and which give rise to ideas, their historical developments and benefits as well as inadequacies. In a secular world, the passionate religious conflicts that characterised most of European history before the nineteenth century, seem to have largely disappeared with a few exceptions such as Northern Ireland. The Catholics and Protestants are no longer engaged in bloody wars against each other. The Christians are not crusading against the Muslims or Jews or even the 'Pagans'.

Islamic countries have not accepted secularism. They have different versions of Islamic polity. Some such as Iran have an Islamic democratic system while others such as Saudi Arabia have monarchical systems. In Islamic countries, wars between the various schisms of Islam have started to get bigger and destructive. Quite a few Islamic groups are engaged in what they call 'jihad' against the West. There are tensions between Jews and Muslims in the Middle East that have been going on for seventy years. There are also tensions between a resurgent Hinduism and Islam in South Asia. The Chinese are trying to lead Muslim Uyghurs into a more secular polity. There are also conflicts in Africa based on religion.

Secularism has not quite made the world peaceful in other regions. Extremely bloody conflicts around nationalism continue in many parts of the world. Secular Superpowers are engaged in both building dangerous weapons and proxy wars. The world is close to the brink of major disasters with almost irretrievable climate change and environmental destruction. Conflicts between different ethnicities are rising and racism continues unabated in even the most developed countries. Hunger and poverty still impact on a large percentage of the world population. Human rights violations have not seen any significant reduction. Inequality persists in every sector of life and economics. The wealth gap between the poor and the rich is growing.

Democracy has not ended marginalisation of minorities. In fact, in many countries, including the most developed countries, minorities and some racial groups have suffered at the hands of populist majoritarian outcomes. Divisions within countries have taken new forms with communities entrenched against each other in democratic systems.

It would appear, that after two world wars in which more people died in wars than in almost all of human history, and in subsequent ethnic wars that have also consumed millions of lives, secularism and liberal democracy have not been quite the nirvana that they were hoped to be. Secular liberal democracy may have helped one region of the world, that is the Occident or what is called west, as it has largely been devoid of wars after 1948, but that region has been active in exporting wars to other parts of the world as well as inflicting inequalities. Therefore, there is a need to look at other options of governance and human relations based on different concepts.

This section briefly looks at two aspects; first around consensus, whether the Sikh perspective on consensus is built around simple democracy or if it is uniquely sophisticated to reduce tensions in society. The second looks at the political philosophy of secularism and whether GurSikhi has a different perspective. Finally, the section examines whether Sri Akal Takht Sahib devoid of any political or legal shadow over it offers a better opportunity to explore and develop these than existing institutions.

CONSENSUS
DECISION MAKING AND ACCOUNTABILITY AT SRI AKAL TAKHT SAHIB, SARBAT KHALSA

Collective decisions are ideally made at Sri Akal Takht Sahib in an assembly of Sikhs called the Sarbat Khalsa. It is inaugurated under a Jathedar who effectively becomes the spokesperson as well as the chosen representative to build consensus in the assembly. The role however has become wider. Essentially the Jathedar builds consensus on major issues among Sikhs, arbitrates in matters of interpretation and acts as the spokesperson of the Sikhs. The Jathedar does not have the infallible status of the Roman Catholic Pope. The institution of Sarbat Khalsa however enjoys that privilege when gathered and making a decision by consensus at Sri Akal Takht Sahib in the presence of and in accordance with Sri Guru Granth Sahib.

Sri Akal Takht Sahib is ideally the seat from where decisions are announced by the representative or spokesperson or the head of the Sarbat Khalsa who is the Jathedar of Sri Akal Takht Sahib.

The Jathedar is tasked with building consensus. The question is who engages in the decision-making process and who decides who does what. These are questions that have to be worked on in modern times since the Sikhs are no longer concentrated in one region and numerically are in far larger numbers than in the seventeenth century. During the eighteenth century Misl period, before Maharaja Ranjit Singh, the Sarbat Khalsa is considered to have been generally constituted of all the Amritdhari Sikhs who could make their way to the gathering. They went as groups or Misls and generally tended to engage from a collective position of their group or Misl. The Misl heads and leaders of smaller groups often made the decision on behalf of their group or in many cases discussed it among their key members. The period of the Misls was an unsettled time when many either remained in the forests or had just about acquired control over some land. Some like the Nihang Misl refused to become rulers over a land mass and remained a wandering Misl with tremendous influence and respect among the Sikhs. It was seen as a group that gave selfless service to the Sikh Panth. Generally, the Jathedar was chosen from among them as they had no vested interest in defending a territory or occupying one. It was a form of avoidance of conflict of interest.

When Sikhs finally managed to establish a Kingdom under Maharaja Ranjit Singh, they had the opportunity to make the institution of Sarbat Khalsa a well organised, disciplined, informed and representative assembly to reflect the new status of Sikhs as a settling community no longer in perpetual conflict with rulers. Ranjit Singh however dismissed the Sarbat Khalsa. With that ended any hope of keeping the Sarbat Khalsa as a permanent representative and consensus developing democratic institution of the Sikhs for the future. It also ended the opportunity to establish a unique institution based on GurSikhi and Sikh practices.

The Sarbat Khalsa of 1920 was the next major gathering. It led to constructive decisions. It decided on the setting up of two enduring organisations both of which had a significant and long lasting impact. On 15th November 1920, the Shiromani Gurdwara Parbhandik Committee (SGPC) was set up and on 14th December 1920, Shiromani Akali Dal was announced. The SGPC was set up to manage Sikh Gurdwaras while Akali Dal was established as the political body of Sikhs to negotiate with the British colonial power and other political bodies. This was a time when nationwide movements had started efforts to end British rule or at least seek greater representation for Indians. The distinct communities were trying to ensure that they were all represented. The resolutions and the setting up of the two bodies led to the reviving of

Sikh polity, ambition, decision making and empowerment. A major decision taken at the 1920 Sarbat Khalsa was to reclaim management control of all historic Sikh Gurdwaras back into the community. These Gurdwaras had mostly been taken over by individuals who treated them as hereditary properties and who were protected by the British. In their formative years, the two organisations took on the British through peaceful protests and sacrifices, and succeeded. The success of this peaceful movement also gave Sikhs considerable power in the 'independence' movement.

However, the possibility of the Sarbat Khalsa being revived as an institutionalised representative and perpetual Sikh Assembly was displaced by the SGPC which became a democratic forum with members directly elected by Sikhs under State supervision and subject to State prerogatives. In 1925, the SGPC was recognised as a legal statutory body described as the Board in the Gurdwara Act 1925. After 1947, it was justified under Article 25 of the Indian Constitution. The drawback of SGPC that was and remains is that it is a body empowered under a State Act and is a statutory body rather than an independent body of the Sikhs.

It would have been better to have retained and developed the institution of Sarbat Khalsa as a distinct, separate and independent Assembly with a system to help appoint and assist the Jathedar independently of the SGPC. This would have maintained the office of the Jathedar of Sri Akal Takht Sahib free from political pressure and direct intervention. It would also have enabled Sri Akal Takht Sahib to be representative of changing demographics, modern methods and needs. At the same time, the SGPC, once having been enacted by law, should have been limited to managing Gurdwaras and Sikh Shrines, that is, to remain active in 'secular' aspects of a religion as detailed above and empowered under the Constitution.

The SGPC has in fact de-facto taken over the role of the Sarbat Khalsa although its legal status does not permit it to do so. It is also a body restricted to representation in Punjab mainly, disenfranchising Sikhs outside Punjab in decision making. Moreover, over time the Akali Dal, which has gained political power in Punjab on several occasions, dominates SGPC, thus directing its decisions.

Historically, after the tenth Guru, accountability of decisions at Sri Akal Takht have been to the wider Sikh community, now Global Sikh Community. These have been to the Sarbat Khalsa. Hence any pronouncements by the Jathedar are accountable ultimately to the Sarbat Khalsa for their veracity, consistency with Sri Guru Granth Sahib and for their common interest to benefit the Sikhs. This unfortunately was usurped by the SGPC, which has been sanctioning and censoring the decisions and has even resorted to removing Jathedars when decisions or pronouncements have been considered not to be consistent with their interests.

CURRENT CONSENSUS FORMATION IN SIKH INSTITUTIONS

Sikhs have generally been following the British democratic model, known as the Westminster model, that is a first past the post, majoritarian democratic system when consensus of Sangat is sought. This system was influenced by the British during colonialism. In institutions led by 'Sadhus and Sants' there is no attempt to seek consensus from the Sangat. These institutions, sometimes called 'deras', are based on the assumption that the Sadhu or Sant is equivalent of a Brahmgyani (enlightened being) and does not need any advice as he/she is 'all knowing'. Following a Sadh or Sant is a voluntary decision. Hence it can be said that a form of consensus does exist. In theory, followers are not tied by any economic, social or political compulsions to be linked to the dera. They associate by free will.

The majority of Sikh institutions have a system of elections based on the British majoritarian first past the post winner. Elections determine the outcome based on simple majority. Whoever wins the majority then leads for a fixed period. This is a reasonable system in politics where secular issues such as economics, welfare, spending, education policy, foreign policy, etc, are to be decided. However, it can lead to problems in religious institutions.

Faith is based on unquestioning allegiance to the original teachings. The teachings of a religion are left to experts to interpret. They are not meant to be decided by common majoritarian vote. If that happens, the very concept of 'faith' in the scripture and the enlightened being who started the faith, can be undermined if put to a simple majority vote.

For instance, the potential danger in a Sikh religious institution is that the majority may decide that it should no longer be necessary to cover one's head in a Gurdwara. In a majoritarian system in some democratic countries in the world, the law will accept this to be a 'democratic' decision irrespective of whether the higher religious authorities of the religion consider it as unacceptable. A form of this has happened in a Gurdwara in Canada where chairs to sit on were introduced in the main darbar (hall) of the Gurdwara.

A second and insidious effect of simple majoritarian democracy is the fact that any democracy requires at least two people to stand against each other. Both people are in a contest to outdo each other. They can either campaign around their own attributes, assets and abilities, or they can campaign negatively by condemning the character and incompetence of the opposition. In most democratic elections, even in Gurdwaras, the candidates do both. They exaggerate their abilities and their manifestoes while criticising the competing party, sometimes quite vocally, employing dirty tricks. Often potential supporters are encouraged to vote for a candidate by offer of inducements. In some elections this has taken the form of alcohol and drugs too. This, as any observer will infer, is simply not something a religious institution should get into. Adversarial elections by nature bring the best and the worst in candidates.

An election based on a majority voting system also divides the 'sangat' (congregation). This system defeats the very concept of 'sangat' or congregation. Both words mean coming together as a single collective entity in the presence of a scripture, prayer, entity, etc. Congregate means to come together. Sangat means a group of likeminded people which in the context of the Gurdwara is the Sikhs in unity with the Guru, in harmony, in observance together and in humility collectively in the presence of the Guru (Guru Granth Sahib). An election system however creates division, acrimony, insults, parties within the 'sangat' and tensions. It subverts the purpose of the Gurdwara as a place of 'congregating' in unity. Elections have had their effect on Sikh religious institutions and organisations. They have often led to focus on politics, scheming, vitriolic attacks upon each other, divisions and inefficiency in the Gurmat (Guru's teachings) mission of the Gurdwara or organisation.

Sikh institutions that have adopted Westminster form of democratic system include some of the most powerful Sikh organisations, for example, the Shiromani Gurdwara Parbhandik Committee and many major Gurdwaras around the world. There are hustings and all sorts of practices that the world is now used to in any democratic election. In fact, sometimes it becomes quite under hand. Substantial amount of money is spent on these elections.

Voters in most Gurdwara elections have simply to be a 'Sikh'. They do not need to understand or be knowledgeable about GurSikhi. They do not need to be Amritdharis (initiated into greater commitment).

Not surprisingly, the outcome of elections is based on populism and affiliation to a group, a candidate or inducements rather than the suitability of the candidate to promote GurSikhi, the teachings of the Gurus and the welfare of the Sikhs as a community following the Gurus. This is also the case in the elections of the Shiromani Gurdwara Parbhandik Committee (SGPC).

SGPC elections are like any political elections. They have politics, slander, promises, inducements and large costs. They have almost everything except what the candidates will do to promote GurSikhi. The SGPC decides the collective budget of the largest Sikh institutions in Punjab. The institutional and political structure of SGPC has led to many divisions within Sikhs with different groups competing to gain control of it for political and financial reasons. Instead of the different schools of thought coming to a common understanding, the electoral system has driven deeper wedges between different interest groups and schisms within the Sikh community.

Even if the Sikhs wish to transform the electoral system to reflect the teachings of the Gurus, the SGPC election system cannot be changed by Sikhs. This is the prerogative of the Indian Parliament since SGPC as a body is enacted under the Gurdwara Act. It is therefore a statutory body of the State. Any change in its constitution or function has to be approved by the Indian Parliament.

The current election system also impacts on the appointment of the Jathedar and the functioning of Sri Akal Takht Sahib. As SGPC is a politically instituted body and has taken upon itself to appoint the Jathedar of Sri Akal Takht Sahib, it is inevitable that the appointment will be a political one rather than one based on merit or consensus of the wider Sikh community. And as the Jathedar is essentially a political appointee, they become aligned to the party responsible for their appointment. Even if the Jathedar wanted to change the system of consensus building within Sikhs, they are unable to do so because they have to ask the political group that installed them in the position. The political group in turn has to be sensitive to the concerns of the Indian State that ultimately decides when elections are to be held. The elections are generally held when the State is certain that the party that takes control of SGPC will not seek to disrupt the system.

It can be said that ever since the election system was introduced within Sikhs, the number of divisions and schisms within Sikhs has increased. Whether a system based on the principles that the Gurus had taught can be any better is a speculative question. However, if Sri Akal Takht Sahib is free from the constraints of Indian law and politics, an alternative system of consensus to select the Jathedar can be instituted which is consistent with the teachings of the Gurus. It would need to be a consensus of the world-wide Sikh community and would be clearly and purposefully developed with the position and role of the Jathedar.

FORMS OF CONSENSUS

What constitutes consensus at Sri Akal Takht Sahib and what is the institutional organisation of building consensus in GurSikhi?

It is important to appreciate what may be different about democracy, consensus and decision making at Sri Akal Takht Sahib free from any legal or political shadow over it.

Power is always dependent on some form of consensus otherwise it descends into self-destructive despotism and collapses, usually through violence. Consensus takes many forms. It can be between powerful power brokers, warlords, big business interests and other non-democratic forces. This was the structure of power generally in the world at the time of the Gurus. Powerful Monarchs, the Mughals or Maharajahs depended on smaller rulers to support their rule. The support varied from willing consent by some to contractual relations by others who may have been defeated or saw benefit to negotiate protection from a larger ruler. This was the form of rule in India from ancient times. It was the same in most parts of the world, with some periods of democratic interludes as in Greece.

Another form of consensus is the consent given by people to a ruler or decision making process. In ancient times and even in some cultures during Middle Ages this took the form of round tables of nobles, elders or representatives. In some indigenous tribes, the consensus making process is wider within the community.

Parliamentary democracy as a form of consensus Governance was institutionally established by Britain. It was an effort to end English civil wars and is based on the English adversarial culture when two or more competing forces fight until a winner emerges. The winner takes all. English wars were bloody and usually fought till a decisive winner emerged. The winner takes all approach is the basis of British Parliamentary system. The citizens vote. The party that gains the majority, reigns for up to five years or until a Parliamentary coup disposes the leader or the party. The Party that can prove to be 51% or more of the parliamentary vote, gets the power. If the outcome is not smooth or clear, then the Party in power can dissolve Parliament and call for another election to have a clearer majority mandate from the voters.

Some countries have more complex and nuanced democratic systems. They have seats allocated to minorities and minority parties. The complex system often leads to a coalition of various political interests working together to form Government. The advantage of this system is that it largely gets around Tocqueville's description of democracy as the 'tyranny of the 51 against the 49'. By having a coalition, it broadens the political outlook of the Government. The drawback is that Government can be indecisive at times. However, in most countries with complex forms of democratic systems, such as proportional representation in Germany, the Governing system has proven to be representative of a larger percentage of the people. Consensus is also based on positive rather than negative voting. This means that almost all people vote for the issue and the party they directly support rather than against a party they do not like as often happens in tactical voting. These systems have proven to be more stable with fewer disruptions in long term policies and planning. However, in some cases, the Government can take some time in forming as parties negotiate their policies. One of the longest was in Belgium where it took eighteen months to form a government in 2020. But there was no discernible disruption in the country.

Another system is a form of consensus that seeks near unanimity in decision making. This was often the form of consensus in some ancient types of round table assemblies, or in South Asia, the Panchayats. The Pushtoons of Afghanistan have had this form of decision making system for centuries. The disadvantage is that near unanimous consensus can take days if not months if a few people persist in dissenting. The advantage is that once consensus is achieved, the whole tribe or community is committed to the decision without endless opposition within the group.

Hence consensus forming takes different forms. Most Sikh institutions in twentieth century onwards followed British democracy's majoritarian approach. This has sometimes created problems within religious places such as Gurdwaras and religious bodies such as Shiromani Gurdwara Parbhandik Committee. Before twentieth century, the Sikhs had a form of near unanimous consensus forming, called 'Sarb Samti'.

SARB SAMATI - A SIKH FORM OF CONSENSUS

The Gurus had stressed for the Sangat to remain united, to find ways to remove their differences and seek the good in others. Gurubani emphasises the oneness of all. In majh mahela 5th, Gurubani says, '*leave aside duality (otherness), come together and join the eternal as one*'. But an election does exactly the opposite. It creates the 'other'. It promotes duality, attachment to different propositions, to political office and to a group. In that atmosphere, it is difficult to see how 'oneness' can be fostered. Electioneering can bring out the worst in people if it is not well regulated.

The system of consensus that the Gurus had encouraged was the form that strives at near unanimous consensus called 'Sarb Samti'. It is to be consensus with ethical principles based on the teachings of the Gurus. Consensus has to be for the good of everyone. However, near unanimous consensus can be difficult. It could be achieved within minutes or it can take days and weeks. It requires all the various interests and opinions to compromise and find a common ground. Ideally if everyone has good intentions, then a consensus can be reached. However, if there is mischief, a single person can ensure that unanimous consensus is frustrated. A near unanimous consensus system can have a proportionality factor depending on the nature of the issue being discussed.

A system of principles of consensus within Sikhs was operationally practiced by Sikhs until the twentieth century. These practices served the Sikhs well. They are still present to some extent in ad hoc consensus forming. When Sikhs get together they try and build a very wide consensus. However, when constitutions or legal instruments interfere, then the traditional system is abandoned in favour of the majoritarian democratic election. The result of the election system is evident. The Sikhs remain a highly divided community.

A system of consensus based on the teachings of the Gurus is likely to promote unity and cohesion within the worldwide Sikh community, especially in matters of GurSikhi. Consensus requires various groups to seek compromises, to accept each other's differences and to develop a common platform that enables them to work together. 'Sarb Samti', the Sikh system of decision making literally means unanimous consensus. However, a 100% consensus is impossible in most issues in real life. A system of near unanimous consensus can be constructed that requires differential percentage thresholds for different fields of decision. For instance, it might require 98% consensus on the appointment of Jathedar while needing 80% threshold to decide whether voting on an issue should be transparent or by secret ballot, etc. In some cases it may be as small as 60% threshold. These are suggestions for discussion. This form of differential majorities already exists in some democracies. As an example, some countries require 65 -70% majority for a constitutional change. But a simple majority is deemed sufficient for most other issues.

There are always going to be differences in schools of thought, of interpretations, of ambitions and of interest groups. An important principle of consensus according to 'Sarb Samti' is to co-exist with the differences in a way that enables everyone to agree to some common grounds that are shared by everyone, but the differences remain at the periphery. For instance, in the case of the 'maryada' or Sikh code of life and community, there would be some codifications shared by all as a minimum while each school of interpretation can have some added rules or codes of behaviour. This was the intention when the current 'rehat maryada' (Sikh personal code) was formulated. However, over the years, the divisions have meant that different schismatic schools have sought dominance and hegemony in the community by either rejecting the common rehat maryada or aligning with it. Hegemonic tendencies arise when there is a political compulsion to control a community or institution. Consensus on the other hand deflates this impulse to a large extent.

It is important for Sikhs to construct a workable system of consensus building based on the teachings of the Gurus, the purpose of the institution, Gurdwara, or a guiding body. Any system must promote harmony and cohesion. This can only start to happen if GurSikhi can start to function free from the overriding forces of State politics and legal constraints.

PHILOSOPHY, WESTERN DUALISM AND GURSIKHI

The purpose of any idea, philosophy or belief system is to enhance human understanding of reality and engage in it, or of making human life better, more content or more responsible. A worldview such as GurSikhi has all these aspects. It is a way, a methodology or an approach to perceiving reality, of achieving contentment, of finding a purpose in life, of human relations, of relating with environment, other species and the material world among others. In fact, it can be considered to be a complete and comprehensive framework of a structure of thought that contributes, integrates as well as assimilates ideas. It has its own epistemology and pedagogy.

In a secular world, religions generally concentrate on afterlife as well as conduct in this life that can lead to achieving a desirable ambition for afterlife status. For instance, some religions believe that a pious life led according to the teachings, commandments and concepts of that religion can lead to a person reaching 'heaven' in afterlife. This is a primary focus in the Abrahamic belief systems that are generally termed 'religion'.

Epistemological systems in the East generally tend to be systems of thought and knowledge that not only concentrate on afterlife but also on theories about this life, human industry such as governance and behaviour approaches in this life. In fact, not all Eastern systems believe in an afterlife. Generally, the systems of thought from South Asia are called Dharmic Panths or Dharmas. The word Panth roughly means a path. Dharam is a wide ranging word. It encompasses many aspects of life, such as natural laws, behaviour according to the value systems of the Panth, metaphysical concepts and so on. Eastern systems, and consequently GurSikhi, do not just concentrate on 'after life' but are composite systems of thought that do not treat this life and any afterlife as distinctly separable. In most cases Dharmic Panths are methodologies towards comprehending the ultimate reality, relationship and knowledge of all that exists and does not yet exist.

A composite system also means it has unique ideas on everyday issues, such as, ethics, human relations, politics, law, social welfare, social economics, science, development, environment, animal life, communities, coexistence, etc. GurSikhi too has concepts on these aspects of human life. However, they remain unarticulated and unapplied.

The application of GurSikhi in everyday temporal Governance, ethics, economics, jurisprudence, scientific methodology, etc, remains unarticulated and undeveloped. It is not that there is a GurSikhi theory of economics. There is no specific theory of economics in Sri Guru Granth Sahib, nor of politics or jurisprudence. However, there are concepts and ethics, responsibilities and principles, that GurSikhi inspires in systems of Governance, commerce, law and other fields of human relations. Every humanities theory has to recognise values as central to its proposition. For instance, a theory of economics will not simply concentrate on GDP (Gross Domestic Product) but also on how many people the theory pulls out of poverty, etc, and whether it leads to contentment rather than enrichment and whether it offers people opportunity to gain knowledge.

Currently Sikhs are thrust into the bracket of 'religion' and persuaded to concentrate on 'worshipping' within the Occidental epistemological universalism. Where civil society institutions or departments in academic institutions attempt to develop something along the lines of Applied GurSikhi, they usually find institutional restrictions, reduced funding or other cul de sacs that prevent the project from developing.

In contrast, the 'dharmic' system called Hinduism has morphed into an evolving worldview under the name Hindutva. A number of institutions have emerged under the auspices of the Indian State as have various independent organisations and philanthropists that engage in scholarly interpretations of the corpus of texts that form Hinduism. These academic exercises attempt to create a 'Hindu' worldview of ethics, economic principles, political theories and even metaphysics. Hindutva intends to replace the incomprehensible 'Indian Secularism' at some stage in India.

Similar work takes place continuously in some Islamic countries on an Islamic approach to Governance, to economies, to finance, to human rights, to science, to metaphysics, etc. Countries like Iran are at the forefront of a Shia interpretation and worldview. Turkey and Saudi Arabia engage in developing and applying a Sunni Islamic approach to issues of Governance, law, economic theory, etc.

China has set up a number of institutions promoting a Confucius outlook on human relations, human institutions and human systems of Governance.

GurSikhi on the other hand is persuaded to follow the Christian path of focussing on morality, human ethics and afterlife while keeping away from temporal issues such as governance. This is because Sikhs live under jurisdictions that are not of Sikhs. An area where GurSikhi is provided an environment for independent thinking will enable Sikhs to develop a Sikh worldview which could be of immense value to Sikhs and in fact the world.

CONCEPTS FOR OUR TIMES

A substantive challenge that Sikhs face is that GurSikhi has some unique epistemology and pedagogic approach to knowledge and a distinct worldview that needs to be thought out, extrapolated and developed in a changing world where new ideas emerge, new challenges are faced, new scientific theories are proposed, new technological possibilities evolve and different political and social ideologies dominate the public space and State policies. It is important for Sikhs to develop these for themselves and by themselves in a complex and changing world, without restrictions or influences from others. Currently there is no free and politically independent space or a political area where the concepts of GurSikhi can be developed, expressed and manifested as unique but also relevant to everyday life along with guiding an understanding of perennial issues such as the purpose of existence as well as insight into reality.

In the dualist paradigm that has evolved from colonial era and that has been universalised as both certain, logical and 'scientific' based, some of the most profound insights in Guru Granth Sahib are lost in the categorisation of religion. There is no attempt to enquire what is the epistemological structure that leads to these inferences and what is the pedagogic system of way of imparting knowledge that can lead an individual to come to these conclusions without the aid of mechanical gadgetry.

It is worth observing just a few insights conveyed by Guru Nanak. The first is that there are thousands of universes. What was the reasoning, insight, intuition or another method of knowledge acquisition that led to this conclusion. Further there is assertion that time is subjective and finite. As an object emerges in 'time' it then also has an end as will planets and universes, but new cycles begin. There is a statement that there are ten dimensions of which the tenth is beyond comprehension, beyond the limits of time and from where all becomes clear. There is the idea of evolution and water as the source of evolutionary journey on earth. There is also the teaching that reality is the entirety of that which is constructed from matter or materials that can be visualised or perceived and that which cannot be visualised and occupies the space in which no matter exists. The Guru Granth Sahib also talks about chaos and order as intricately linked.

The immediate question that arises is how did Guru Nanak and subsequent Gurus arrive at these conclusions without the aid of gigantic telescopes, Einstein's theory, laboratory to experiment in and mathematical logic. These are propositions in the Guru Granth Sahib long before Darwin, Einstein or Telescopes came on the scene. One idea can be considered to be a work of guessing and coincidence, but to get so many facts that are only now becoming evident in Occidental based knowledge systems is not coincidental but are definitely inferences reached from a different epistemological system and the pedagogy of Sri Guru Granth Sahib is substantially different than the dualist framework of Occidental system of knowledge.

If understood from within the Occidental framework of knowledge then the response would be that Guru Nanak was a man of God or God himself and therefore knew all this. However the Gurus have also said that the knowledge they acquired can be also be gained by anyone who follows their path to that knowledge. What is that path. What is the system of gaining knowledge of reality and what is the passage of transference of that knowledge from Guru Granth Sahib to the seeker? This can certainly not be understood or explained within the dualist Occidental construction of knowledge and system of knowledge production.

Some of the insights expressed in Sri Guru Granth Sahib also exist in a few ancient knowledge systems in South Asia. Unfortunately these have all been lumped as Hinduism within the Occidental framework. This is despite the fact that the word Hindu does not exist in the Vedas or the Upanishads and is generally thought to have been coined by the Arabs. The epistemology and pedagogy within some pre GurSikhi philosophies have also been confused and lost within the political word Hindu, the religious category Hinduism and the civilisation Hindu.

The recovery of the epistemological system and pedagogy of knowledge cannot realistically happen within a distinct Sikh State that might be established along current State theory, an autonomous Sikh dominated region subject to a political system that is not Sikh in origin or within current secular or theocratic political systems around the world. It can be possible at Sri Akal Takht Sahib and under its auspices independent of any jurisdiction or political shadow in time as independent questions are asked and independent thinking outside the framework of occidental universalism starts to develop.

Most of the world now follows secular ideology as a political system, and human social ideas that have emanated from a few countries from the Occident, with the exception of many Islamic countries that have a theocratic governance. The secular system categorises non secular ideologies and non dualist worldviews as religion or belief and marginalises them into the personal domain. It is a colonial legacy.

The secular political system creates some problems too. An important feature of GurSikhi is that it is a comprehensive system of knowledge and there is no distinction between secular and the religious. In fact these words are meaningless within the knowledge base of Guru Granth Sahib. GurSikhi is a worldview that integrates both. Further development of this worldview is difficult to evolve from within either a secular environment or a theocratic one. It is important to understand the challenges and why it is difficult and ask the question whether GurSikhi can survive as a unique worldview and thrive in a secular polity and what is different or unique about Sikhi.

CAN GURSIKHI SURVIVE AND THRIVE UNDER SECULARISM?

Can GurSikhi survive and thrive and be free to express itself in the modern secular State and polity? Secularism allegedly provides the space for freedom of religion. However, it does not provide the opportunity for expression of nonsecular worldviews, categorised as 'religion', in the public sphere or in State matters. A non dualist system categorised as religion therefore has to be treated as a personal matter between an individual and his/her belief. There are two problems here. The first is the forced imposition of the category of 'religion' upon Indic worldviews, in this case GurSikhi. The second is that even if GurSikhi was given a broader appreciation as a 'dharam' or worldview with a particular belief system in any country, secularism is too restrictive a political philosophy to enable GurSikhi an opportunity to develop and express its pluralistic approach as well as engage properly in the public sphere. It is worth understanding what is secularism, how it evolved and what is its passion.

GENESIS OF MODERN SECULARISM

Modern secularism is essentially a western development in reaction to the centuries of Christiandom, an age in which there was little if any tolerance of the diversity of schisms within Christianity let alone other belief systems, ideas and worldviews. Secularism brought tolerance of some plurality to western civilisation and led to tremendous development in technology, medicine, science, human rights and representative governance.

Secularism as a philosophy is considered to have evolved from the Christian concept of the seculum, which means a finite age or temporal. It is a Latin word. A belief in duality, the temporal as that of this world and the spiritual as being of the timeless God, gradually led to a division called secular and religious, State and Church, in Christian doctrines and Christian Europe or rather modern Europe.

For a long time the political, legal and social order was dictated by Christian doctrine in Europe with the Church dominating ethical and political sphere of everyday life. However, schisms in Christianity led to wars between the different interpretations. Moreover, the other Abrahamic religions, Judaism and Islam, were in constant struggle with Christianity. The basis of these conflicts is in the original claim of Abrahamic traditions. All three religions believe that they have inherited the genuine message from God. Christianity and Islam both believe that they are the one and true 'revelation' for all human beings intended by God. They each have a passionate belief in the authenticity of their own belief system at the exclusion of others, leaving little room for tolerance let alone pluralistic coexistence. Judaism however does not make a pretence to be universalist for all the world but restricts its claim to within Jews. It is not intolerant of other beliefs even if it excludes them in history. Politically, Judaism did not seek to marginalise other beliefs except among Jews.

It is Christianity and Islam that make wider claims to be the 'authentic' revelations of God for all of humanity. As a result of the absolutist nature of these beliefs, they have also fought over hundreds of years with each other, with others and even within their own religious communities who differed from interpretations of a powerful group that sought to impose its interpretation of the 'absolute' truth upon other schisms.

Christian rule did not tolerate other worldviews and alternative beliefs or religions in its domain nor did it accept metaphysical theories that contradicted its own ideas. The position of the Medieval Christian Church was antagonistic to theories that emerged from scientific observations such as that the earth rotates around the sun. European civilisation dealt with its constant internal conflicts between different Christian interpretations and the obstructive attitude of the Christian Church to developing scientific knowledge by excising religion from the sphere of politics, knowledge and legal systems. Up to the medieval period in Europe, the nature and politics of the State, the basis of law and publicly accepted 'knowledge' was determined by religious doctrine. But the revolution against the tyranny of the Church or rather the growing acceptance of science and rebellion against Church absolutism overturned this and religious doctrine was marginalised from the system of public knowledge to idiosyncratic 'personal belief'. This movement or rather 'revolution' against Christendom became consolidated in the nineteenth and twentieth centuries. Thus Christianity was no longer the source of 'knowledge' by which human society advanced. It was relegated to the same category as horoscopes, as mere belief. Due to its historically very powerful hold on society and its extremely influential institutions, the Christian Church retained a far more influential status in State and society than an astrologer, but the principal category it was boxed into, that is, a 'belief', is almost the same for both. Christianity increasingly began to be called 'religion' rather than knowledge, a 'belief' rather than fact.

Conventionally, in the west religion has become a matter of personal faith pursued by people in their private lives. Religion no longer informs or rather dominates State policy or education system. Nor does it have any sanction over science. The philosophy that determines public policy is called secularism which essentially means negation of religion in the public sphere. Secularism is of this world with no reference to God or eternal metaphysical concepts of Christianity. The domain of these fields came to be called religion or belief. In simple terms, life on earth became a person's world while the afterlife, etc, became God's world. The two are not to interfere with each other's domains. Secularism was a settlement or rather a compromise between the political power of the institutions representing the two worlds. In terms of knowledge, secularism empowers 'scientific thinking' (whatever that is) but tolerates non scientific beliefs without incorporating them in essential policy or knowledge.

In theory, secularists say all religions are treated equally and the State respects everyone's right to a personal religion. However, it is not so simple. The secular does not mean equality of all religions, etc. The religion of the majority has either overt or subtle influence in the way the 'secular' is interpreted and applied. Often the ethics and treatment of 'others' or minorities and their belief systems are determined by the influence of the majority religion in the secular.

This is evident both in France and in India. In France, Catholicism enjoys considerable privileges although it may not be seen to be determining public policy. It is in India where the secular takes on a different perspective often called 'Indian secularism'. There is no such word as Indian secularism defined in any dictionary. It is a rhetorical invention by Indian politicians. There is no well defined or articulated political theory called 'Indian secularism'. There are no texts that give an understanding of Indian secularism or offer a theoretical framework from which to draw ideas of democratic institution, rights, privileges, etc, that can be considered to be derivatives of 'Indian secularism'.

The statement by Indian politicians and some academics that Indian secularism is 'equal treatment' of all religions is not a position that is assumed in the Indian Constitution or supported in Indian Supreme Court decisions. If there is equal treatment, it is a negative equality. It is theoretically the equal negation or exclusion of all religions from State function. Nevertheless, as many academics have said, there is never a completely neutral public space, even more so in India where the State has legislated frequently in favour of majority 'Hindu' religion and acted against minority religions. In some cases, political parties in India have legislated to protect idiosyncratic outdated practices of some minorities to ensure their votes. The secular State, particularly the democratic one, often tends to lean towards the majority religion as those in power are dependent upon appeasing the majority for their votes. Hence in India the word Indian secularism effectively means a compromise between western secularism and political challenges posed by indigenous beliefs. It is not uniformly applied. Those with significant voting or other clout tend to succeed in forcing compromises.

The division of the secular and religious gave rise to tremendous advances in Occidental civilisation as it freed it from the moralising, theological and restrictive positions of Christian Church. One of the consequences of the rise of secularism as an ideology in the Occident and its export around the world through colonial education has been to classify all non secular philosophies, worldviews and concepts as 'religions, faiths or beliefs'. Just as the Abrahamic traditions and particularly traditional Christianity have been universalist in their claim to know the 'one and only truth', secularism has inherited this universalising phenomenon and assumes that only secularism guarantees freedom of conscience, human development and scientific based knowledge. This has successfully displaced many alternative worldviews and philosophies from the public sphere even when they do not lead to the consequences of aggressive competition and 'the only truth' assertion of Abrahamic traditions. Even though many non-Abrahamic traditions did not suppress scientific knowledge or freedom of expression, they found themselves pushed into the duality of private and public sphere perceived from a European template of history. European history, experience and outcome has been universalised with disregard to whether other parts of the world had similar baggage or problems.

THE LIMITING EFFECT OF THE SECULAR ON GURSIKHI

As a pluralistic philosophy, GurSikhi promotes the concept of coexistence of diversity of ideas, cultures and people. GurSikhi does not provoke proselytising nor does it make sole claims to all truth. GurSikhi does not seek to universalise itself over all others. This was evident in the one major Kingdom ruled by a Sikh Maharajah. It was an exemplary State of diversity and pluralism. Consequently, the secular as a solution to religious conflicts in the public domain has no evolutionary relevance in a Sikh worldview particularly when the development of secularism is considered in the context of European history as an antidote to religious conflicts between religions and between schisms. In the Sikh concept of a plural world, even atheism, although often alleged as contradictory to Sikh philosophy, has legitimate right to exist as an alternative form of thought. However, although GurSikhi can survive within secularism, can it thrive in a secular polity? The question is between surviving and thriving. It is appropriate to appreciate the limitations of a secular system and whether it is a necessary political order for Indic traditions, particularly GurSikhi. An equally important question is whether GurSikhi is disenfranchised as a worldview within the limiting boundaries of secularism.

The duality of secularism and classification of GurSikhi as a religion has been a disruptive influence for GurSikhi and the Sikhs. It has created a self inflicted confusion and begs the question whether western dualistic approach is consistent with GurSikhi and whether GurSikhi can really breathe freely or develop as a comprehensive world view in a secular State.

In GurSikhi, like some other Indic traditions, the temporal and the spiritual are all part of the same reality. They are not two divisible domains. The Creation and the Creator are not separate but all of Creation is the existential manifestation of the Creator according to GurSikhi. Therefore, there is nothing in space and time that belongs solely to human beings and nothing which is outside the presence of the Creator. In fact, in the context of Indic traditions, the word religion does not explain anything about them and neither does the word secular explain anything that it can contrast with. The overall term used for the truth that Indian traditions seek is Dharma and the traditions themselves are 'panths' or paths. Dharma is quite a complex word. It incorporates belief, ethics, philosophy, metaphysical ideas, human relations and many additional characteristics. The various panths seek an understanding of the ultimate truth. According to many South Asian 'panths', knowledge of the ultimate truth can neither be articulated in human language nor communicated in any form through human forms of communication. This also means that an 'ultimate truth' cannot be imposed upon others since there is no way of communicating its understanding. The word secular does not have any substantive meaning or convey any conceptual alternative as a political or legal framework in most Indian traditions since there is no absolutist 'religion' trying to universalise itself or denounce or condemn 'scientific' knowledge. In fact, the scientific method is very much part of some Indic traditions, such as GurSikhi, in deciphering mechanistic knowledge.

The secular as a public domain free of religious, the spiritual, etc, is a meaningless statement in GurSikhi because the duality of temporal and religious does not resonate with Sikh philosophy or concepts nor are there historic circumstances which require its necessity. Sikhs do not make sole claim to the truth. GurSikhi holds that the human is fallible and therefore liable to misinterpret the given truth of any revelation, knowledge or 'divine' intuition. As a result, GurSikhi promotes pluralism. Secularists and atheists can co-exist in the Sikh worldview but cannot solely dominate the public domain anymore than others. Hence, the scope for religious conflicts based on a staunch belief in one's truth as the only universal truth does not arise from GurSikhi in the Sikh proposal of Governance. The idea of belief in a 'God that bodes no other gods' is not part of Sikh belief system.

GurSikhi does not restrict scientific research or its theories in anyway except where the public good or welfare is affected. GurSikhi is neither an obstacle to development nor does it restrict free thinking. Consequently, there is no need to introduce secularism in Sikh polity or impose secularism upon Sikhs since it is irrelevant. It would appear that thinkers in India who adopted secularism seemed to have first internalised and then transplanted or grafted European historic experience upon Indian civilisation without critical analysis. In other words, they assumed, without any empirical evidence, that India was going to explode in similar ways to medieval Europe if its own traditional non dual and pluralistic philosophy formed the basis of its political and constitutional system. It is important to appreciate that the evolution of GurSikhi and Sikh history prior to colonialism was independent of any European influences.

In an Occidental universalised secular environment, GurSikhi cannot evolve as a holistic concept. Ideas from GurSikhi, whether in politics, social or in the wider pursuit of knowledge are limited by restricting its stature to merely a personal belief system. In fact, apart from 'worshipping' or some thinkers writing books and articles from its core concepts, its value to the world is restricted by it being termed religion. Any ideas that Sikhs may think of in fields other than personal religion are fragmented by the secular into 'religious' and secular and consequently made irrelevant in the public sphere. Any books on Sikh thought are displayed on shelves in religion category in bookshops and libraries rather than in the general stalls on different knowledge systems. While Sikhs can thrive as individuals or even as a community in secular polity and environment, GurSikhi cannot evolve or experiment with its ideas beyond the private lives of Sikhs or in the Gurdwaras. While GurSikhi can survive in a western secular environment, it cannot thrive or evolve or its knowledge be successfully transmitted. Hence it needs a place where its ideas can be freely allowed expression without being atomised into secular and religious.

THE SCOPE OF GURSIKHI UNDER 'INDIAN SECULARISM'

The violence at partition of the subcontinent into India and Pakistan in 1947 has been cited as the reason for introducing secularism in India. But it is not a persuasive enough argument in favour of imposing secularism in India. The communal violence was partly engineered, but was mostly a result of poor comprehension of by colonials and their misinformed approach to political representation in South Asia. The Governance structures introduced by British colonialism encouraged communalism within society. Partition was also badly managed by the colonial power. The British failed to plan for it and once the violence started, the British officers failed to control it with the deployment of police and army. To abandon the concepts of Indian civilisation because of an aberration in its long history of one major communal conflict and that also as a consequence of management by a non Indian ruler, reveals a weakness of conviction and a decision taken under a state of panic and fear, possibly even a lack of indigenous intellectual propositions at the time which failed to critically evaluate a colonial worldview. If a similar decision were to have been made in Europe as a result of the 50 million deaths in the Second World War, then post war Europe should have abandoned secular politics and returned to theocratic Statecraft since both Nazism and liberal democracy are secular creations. They led to more destruction and deaths than all of Christiandom did in history.

Duality as a philosophy is not completely alien to Indian traditions. In fact, the Samkhya school is one such dualistic school that has coexisted with other schools such as Advaita and Nyaya in Indian history. They have thrived side by side without conflict. Indian political tradition permits individuals and schools of thoughts to deviate from the mainstream nondual philosophies without sanction, judgement or persecution. The nondualist systems of Governance in Indian traditions were not hostile or a threat to Samkhya. But what is new about modern India is the preference in and domination of the public sphere by this school at the expense of the other. Metaphorically it can be said that Samkhya, which was a minor school of thought, has been elevated to State philosophy since Samkhya and secularism have a lot in common. In fact, it can even be suggested that it is the Carvaka school which has finally triumphed in the contemporary public domain even though it had allegedly disappeared in the eighteenth century. The Carvaka school does not recognise any grand plan (pre-determination) in the lives of people, life after death or even the idea of the soul.

Secularism in India is a radical and unnecessary departure from the long tradition of Indian civilisation. It has not worked. While the constitution, legal and executive administration assumes a secular bias, realpolitik in India has been highly communalised. Labelling Indian Dharmic traditions as religion and forcing them into the margins has been a failure. Inherent in most Indic traditions is their role in the public sphere. Instinctively these traditions attempt to claw their way back into the public sphere albeit through unfortunate routes and methods. They have had to compete and assert themselves through competitive politics. The result is communal violence and politicisation of Indian traditions whereas once they used to coexist as partners in the public space strengthening plurality of thought.

Against this background of a dualist political and philosophical paradigm and a communalised public space where Indic belief systems have been marginalised as religions, GurSikhi is limited to concentrate on 'afterlife' as Abrahamic religions do.

RESISTANCE TO SECULARISATION AND ASSIMILATION

Punjab has defied the trend that was common elsewhere in India. Secularism as the sole claimant to the public domain has repeatedly been resisted more robustly by Sikhs because its assumed necessary benefit and its attempt at dominating the public sphere is irrelevant and antagonistic to Sikh concepts of plurality and diversity.

Ironically, it is not the Sikh intelligentsia, but the Sikhs of the villages who have been most resistant to westernisation and consequently secularisation of Sikh polity. The refusal to reconstruct Sikh polity into purely secular had been the strength and lately the weakness of the Akali Dal. It was Akali Dal's strength because the ordinary Sikh could empathise with the political intuition of the Akali Dal as a party that did not fracture the public sphere with a dualistic worldview of secular and religious. The average Sikh could connect with and feel fully participant in the Akali Dal's campaigns. However, this refusal to become secular also led to its later weakness because the party could not challenge the label of being communal and a party of one community. It could not make a convincing argument for a wider appeal for its political position in an alleged secular political system. The party had not invested in developing conceptual frameworks and intellectual ideas to sustain its position against otherwise powerful secularising political trends. The Akali Dal is unable to justify its existence or evolve policies from a distinctive Sikh perspective because it simply has not invested any effort into developing the concepts that would constitute a Sikh political thought in contrast to secular political theories. Few, if any, of its leadership can articulate the ideas and concepts that differentiate it from other parties. Often it gives the impression of pursuing communal agendas rather than a unique political philosophy. In the end, bereft of a thought out position, it declared itself to be a 'secular' party at a time when its previous national partner BJP (Bharatya Janata Party) is overtly 'Dharmic'. The statement angered many Sikh intellectuals who see it as a betrayal of Akali Dal's original purpose when it was formed in 1920.

Influenced by western and 'Indian secularism' the Sikhs at large have also generally failed to evaluate issues and trends from a Sikh critical perspective. The Sikh intelligentsia generally uses the dominant western (mostly Anglo-Saxon) critique to analyse western hegemonic ideas and interestingly use that analytic framework to evaluate even their own traditions. There are usually attempts to interpret Sikh political thought in the framework of socialism, humanist capitalism, communism, capitalism, activist theology, etc, or whatever is the trend at the time.

The conflict between western form of dualism and Sikh philosophy or concepts has resulted in a number of disturbing and sometimes violent confrontations with the State system in South Asia. This is because the State (India) adopted Western evangelic approach and often sought to impose its preferred and communalised secularity (calling it Indian Secularism) over Sikh polity and forced a change in Sikh perspectives. It has attempted to reconstruct Sikh polity. For instance, the State prefers the Sikhs to forget thinking of themselves in terms of a nation or engage in politics based on Sikh principles. It has wanted Sikhs to think of GurSikhi as a religion of worshipping practised in Gurdwaras and homes and GurSikhi to provide personal moral guidance without any influence in the public sphere of politics and State administration.

The resistance to State machinations has taken on different forms of reactions at different times. The first reaction after the transfer of power in 1947 came in 1951. A brief attempt at merging Sikh polity into national secular politics by disbanding the Akali Dal in 1950 ended with loss of power and the Sikhs feeling deceived. It was felt that while individual Sikhs might do well in secular parties such as in the Congress, the collective Sikh community and the development of Sikh identity and philosophy in a changing world would be greatly compromised because the national Indian Government failed to establish adequate legal protection for minorities from being assimilated or being subservient to majority prerogatives. Akalis reconstituted the Akali Dal as a political party. The second major reaction was the campaign for a Punjabi Suba (linguistic based provincial state) in order to protect the

Sikh script, Gurmukhi, and the conventional common language of the Sikhs, Punjabi. After a 10 year struggle the Sikhs finally managed to form a Punjabi speaking province in India. The survival and promotion of Punjabi (in Gurmukhi script) in the state is considered extremely important by Sikhs for the survival and progress of Sikhi.

However, an uncomfortable relationship between the Sikh regional political party and the central Indian State led to further tensions as the central government continued to extend its remit over regions and obstruct them from realising their own potentials. Moreover, interference in Sikh political affairs led to calls for autonomy for a Sikh dominated provincial state and in fact a federal structure for all Indian states. Sikhs felt that if the powers of the central Government were restricted then the Sikh dominated Punjab state could develop considerably based on ethos of Gursikhi and be free from the communal political mischief of the national political parties. The call for autonomy resulted in further conflict and a violent reaction from the central Government. In 1984 the Indian State's attack on Sri Darbar Sahib (Golden Temple Complex) led to calls for a separate sovereign Sikh State by some Sikhs.

All these reactions were in response to the tensions and conflicts that have resulted between a pluralistic Sikh perspective and the Indian State's preference for the narrower polity of European style secularism. Whenever the Indian State has tried to force secularism upon the Sikhs or interfere in their internal politics, a significant section of Sikhs have responded by starting a movement for demands that challenge the State. Sometimes these demands have been a call for a separate Sikh State. This demand was more often than not a rhetorical response to the State. The unarticulated but self-conscious intention of most Sikhs usually was and continues to be to ward off interference within their internal polity and continue with their non-dualist political approach as well as their way of life.

The attack on Sri Darbar Sahib is significant. While the official version is that the State was trying to stop secession, dealing with terrorism and restoring law and order, the Sikh version is that the State was trying to put the Sikhs in their place, frustrating a peaceful campaign for autonomy and exploiting Sikh politics for electoral gain elsewhere. The underlying compulsions may in fact have been different. In Punjab the Sikh polity has been built on a non-dualist platform. The Congress Government was committed to secularising or rather Europeanising the whole of India. In its worldview, it found Sikh politics to be communal, representing one community, while from a Sikh perspective there was nothing communal in Akali Dal formed along the ideology it was instituted. The Sikhs saw Akali Dal as a natural Indian phenomenon where integration of belief systems and political representation of communities was as intrinsic to Indian civilisation as masala is. They considered politics as a negotiation of interests and coalition of community groups, represented as they viewed Congress as largely Hindu and Akali Dal as largely Sikh. In Government, the Akali Dal adopted a pluralist governance. Nevertheless, there remains ideological conflict between a nationwide party committed to socially engineer Indian civilisation into some version of western secularism or lately in a form of western nationalism on the one hand and a regional party evolved from indigenous civilisation on the other hand.

The most powerful living symbol of the non-dualist approach of Sikhs was and is Sri Akal Takht Sahib. The most powerful institutionalised symbol of Congress party's dualist approach was the Indian Constitution with clear mission to secularise the country. The two were bound to come into conflict some day as was obvious that the Hindu Mahasabha (a Hindu political movement) and the Sangh Parivar (a political coalition of Hindu organisations) was going to challenge the Congress ideology. The Congress dealt with Hindu movements by adopting some of their demands under what it politically termed 'Indian secularism', essentially meaning perverting secularism to gain or hold onto power. With minorities like Sikhs, the Congress ideological machine decided to take them head on. This was the instinctive assessment of many Sikhs who saw the attack on Sri Darbar Sahib in 1984 as an attempt to destroy the political power of the 'Sikhs' as a community. They pointed to the targeted attack on Sri Akal Takht Sahib in 1984 and came to the conclusion that Congress had planned to reduce the significance of Sri Akal Takht Sahib in Sikh political life.

It is relevant to look at the options of the Sikhs and the relevance of Sri Akal Takht Sahib in relation to them if Sikhs want to continue with GurSikhi rather than the hybrid religious entity 'Sikhism' that evolved in twentieth century under the influence of a secular polity. The options are to remain in secular politics with some compromises as followers of a personal religion, or have a Sikh State, or constitute a non-territorial entity with an independent base somewhere. But with the latter two there is a need to find a suitable arrangement with Sri Akal Takht Sahib.

OPTIONS

- THE SOVEREIGNTY OF GURU GRANTH-GURU PANTH
- PERSONAL RELIGION IN A SECULAR STATE
- SURVIVAL OF MIRI PIRI GURSIKHI
- THE IDEA OF A SIKH STATE
- A STATE ON SIKH CONCEPTS
- NON-TERRITORIALITY
- QAUM
- IS THERE A SIKH DIASPORA?
- COMPLICATIONS OF NON-TERRITORIALITY
- CHANGED DEMOGRAPHY OF THE PANTH

THE SOVEREIGNTY OF GURU GRANTH-GURU PANTH

Perhaps the concept of sovereignty in GurSikhi needs to be appreciated to understand the non-territorial nature of Sikh Nation or Sikhs as a People. Sovereignty among Sikhs does not lie in a community based territory. Nor in a person. It is in the combination of Guru Granth and Guru Panth. Guru Granth as the Shabad Guru, its teachings and its concepts, immersed in action within the Global Sikh community following the path of the Gurus; Guru Panth, forms the idea of sovereignty among the Sikhs. It is free of territorial limits and attachments.

The Guru Granth Sahib is the embodiment of the ten Gurus who nurtured, led by example, and gradually evolved GurSikhi to be understandable by the followers over the lifespan of ten Gurus. The Guru Granth Sahib is often called a 'holy book' by non-Sikhs and placed along other religious texts of the world. Guru Granth Sahib in fact is not a 'historical' text. It is a textual embodiment of the ten Gurus and treated as if it is they who are speaking through the text. Guru Granth Sahib is rather a lengthy compilation of concepts which coalesce to present one overarching but quite a complex concept of reality (or ultimate truth) as taught by the ten Gurus. Guru Nanak Dev Ji considered that human language is limited in its ability to relay or describe complex concepts of reality. The Gurus expressed their teachings in poetry. Poetry has the ability to go beyond everyday language in constructing concepts that are otherwise lost in plain language. The poetic teachings of the Gurus are then further recited in raags, an Indian tradition of introducing ambience of emotion, mood, feeling, and what in traditional Indian arts is called 'rass'. This combination of poetry and raag has the effect of creating a state of meditation upon the words of the Gurus, the Guru Granth Sahib on a path to enlightenment.

The Guru Granth Sahib is considered by the Sikhs as a living embodiment rather than a 'book' or 'text' when it is expressed in poetic form and raag. What is called a 'book' or 'holy book' by others is considered a 'living Guru' by the Sikhs. Hence the Sikhs do not treat it as they and the rest of the world would treat a book of texts. Guru Granth Sahib is accorded the respect, the status and the treatment, one would give to a revered living being. It is always placed on a pedestal and when moved, it is held high on the head, covered in clothed protection. The Guru Granth Sahib is not placed on tables, chairs, bags etc as one would with an ordinary book.

The distinctive feature of Guru Granth Sahib is that it is not a historical narrative, nor a proscriptive text of metaphysics. It speaks and engages the individual either alone or in community called the sangat. This becomes part of a shared experience with the Guru. The Guru is present and alive with the individual or community and guiding the individual or community towards comprehending the complexity of reality through a meditative experience.

The Guru becomes part of the individual or the community when the individual or community gets closer to the Guru through the teachings, recitations, and raags. When the individual or community understands that their only guide is the Guru, they become part of the Guru Panth.

It is perhaps the limitation or idiosyncrasy of the English language, that the Guru is being described as 'it'. While the Gurus were all male, the Guru Granth Sahib as their collective embodiment has no gender. Talking of Guru Granth Sahib in gender neutral language is normal in Punjabi, but difficult in English.

Panth literally means path. Guru Panth is the word given to the community that considers the Guru Granth Sahib as its only guide and internalises the Guru in its actions, practices, worldview and life. The Guru Panth accepts no other guide. It is intimately committed to Guru Granth Sahib. The mutual and integrated Guru Granth and Guru Panth is what is considered sovereign in Sikhs. It is not a territory nor is it a throne. It is not a constitution nor a political power over a people. It is both abstract and real. Sovereignty is Guru Granth-Guru Panth. It has no particular place and no particular country. It is not of this world nor of the next. It is a continuum that is not confined in time or space.

The Sikhs as a People coexist in two realities. One is within the jurisprudence of the sovereign Nation-State and the other is in the realm of the Guru Granth-Guru Panth. Sometimes the two collide, raising tensions. Sometimes there is an attempt by States to hem in the Sikhs within their political and jurisprudence ideologies.

The Sikhs who take Amrit (initiation into commitment) become part of the Panth Khalsa. Khalsa is the word given to an Amritdhari Sikh. The wider Sikh community, or Panth, that constitutes Sikhs who are Amritdhari, non Amritdhari, Kesadhari and Patit (not keeping unshorn hair), is generally called Sikh Qaum by Sikhs.

PERSONAL RELIGION IN A SECULAR STATE

Among Sikhs some have tried to promote the western secularist idea of a personal religion and separating the religious from the secular. They consider this as a necessary process for modernising the Sikhs and 'bring' them into the 'real' world. However, the duality of personal religion and the secular public domain creates a form of GurSikhi inconsistent with its teachings and worldview as has been discussed above. Interestingly, the west, as has been evident in USA and UK, is beginning to reallocate some aspects of the public space in decision making for religious institutions after a century of separation. Consequently, the position held by some Sikh intelligentsia that secularisation is 'progressive' and necessary for 'modernisation' would in fact appear to be outdated by two decades at least, particularly as the West itself is beginning to give up this approach. Western development in expanding the public space to re-engage religions is beginning to resemble the Sikh approach.

There can be a personal understanding of reality or a personal variation of religion or a personal choice of a religious doctrine. But to assert that the idiosyncrasy of personal interpretation and choice can only be made in a secular environment and that the broader concept of religion or non-dualist traditions should therefore be taken out of the public domain, its ethical and knowledge systems, is not consistent with logic except through the particular trajectory of European history. People make personal choices in several alternatives offered by the State in the public domain, such as political ideologies, careers, universities and schools, and so on. Similarly, in the Indian civilisation, there is a choice of Dharmic Panths (paths) in the public domain which individuals are free to choose.

As mentioned before, the word 'Dharam' is complex and can incorporate several abstract, metaphysical and normative notions. There are broad Dharmic panths, such as GurSikhi, Vedanta, Jain, Buddhism, etc. There is the Dharam of a person, there is the Dharam of a tree, a horse, a stone, etc, and even the State has a Dharam.

It can well be asked, what is the Dharam of the State? In Indian traditions, the Dharam of the State is common to almost all belief systems. It is not atheist or secular. The state is not without an ethical and political 'soul', responsibilities, duties or even 'persona'. It has to be just; it has to encourage and support people's beliefs; it has to provide basic necessities to people and so on. The State supports all forms of faiths and Dharmic panths and even nurtures them. The State therefore has a positive role in the field of Dharam by encouraging, financially supporting and defending the faiths of the people rather than push it completely out of the public domain and be blind to Dharam in its own functioning remit. Thus, belief and the different Dharmic traditions are not excluded from the public domain. Instead, the State has to be inclusive of the diversity of systems, ensuring their coexistence and free choice while building a consensus on common values and rules of coexistence, in other words, laws, policies and social responsibilities.

A personalised version of GurSikhi may be the only option in Western countries and currently in Indian secular polity, but it will be wrong to state that this is a 'modernising' necessity for Sikhs. It is a compromise or pragmatic approach in a secular polity. A hybrid version of Sikhi, a synthesis between GurSikhi, secular humanism and Protestantism did evolve in the early twentieth century and continues to date under the label 'Sikhism' but it restricts the scope of developing a Sikh worldview. The idea of a personalised religion in a desacralized public domain is a contingent compromise for Sikhs but not ideal for developing ideas, public policy, value systems, etc, from a Sikh perspective.

SURVIVAL OF MIRI PIRI GURSIKHI

It is reasonable to ask whether GurSikhi unconstructed within Occidentalism is a challenge or hostile to every secular or mono-theocratic political system. In fact, the Sikh non-dualistic approach, which is the philosophical context of many eastern philosophies, does not make it difficult for Sikhs to be 'good and constructive citizens' in secular countries, even like India. For individuals or communities of Sikhs, a sound humanitarian secular system is not an antagonistic system to participate in. India is an example where Sikhs have thrived well as individuals and even as a community and lived peacefully until the State has tried to interfere with or exploit the central institutions or concepts of the Sikhs or attempted to convert the body politics of Sikhs into a secularist form.

On the whole India has tried accommodating particular cultural aspects of different communities in its constitutional system with some success despite its 'secular' claim. But from time to time politicians exploit its secular position and use it against minorities or in electoral politics. The Sikhs can coexist successfully and constructively in any secular country as long as the country does not interfere in the internal dynamics and the body polity of the Sikhs. One of the reasons for this is that since the concept of secular does not really exist in GurSikhi, the Sikh philosophy has within it most of the principles that western secularism has given rise to, such as human dignity, freedom of conscience and freedom of opportunity. As long as these principles exist, Sikhs can adapt and coexist without tension except when the State deliberately attempts to reconstruct GurSikhi for political or ideological reasons.

Indeed, that has been the experience of Sikhs around the world. They have successfully engaged in the public sphere of almost all countries without problems. It is when their collective identity and philosophy is under threat that Sikhs feel uncomfortable with the politics of the State.

However, there is a feeling of a collective loss of a core among Sikhs as a people. Sikhs feel that they are unable to contribute to the world as a collective community or even represent themselves as a people in any arena. They feel that Sikh philosophy has much to offer but the space to develop Sikh concepts in relation to the modern world does not exist.

The Sikh philosophy itself cannot evolve, engage and contribute to human organisation when it is pushed into the limited category of religion and subsequently into the personal domain. There are many aspects of GurSikhi which are more inclusive than secular and humanistic philosophies in terms of human organisation and relations. In other words, Sikhs can engage in a secular environment without conflict or in some cases compromise, but GurSikhi itself cannot survive, thrive and make its original contribution under a secular political paradigm as a distinct worldview as it is bracketed into 'religion', restricting its scope. Secularism itself is a limited paradigm.

Further, the lack of a space in which GurSikhi can reinterpret in light of evolving developments in human relations, politics and science has led to a fragmented number of views and strategies. There is not a coherent Sikh perspective that can guide Sikhs across the world and strengthen their commitment to citizenship within the countries they live in or deal with their issues without compromising their principles.

So while Sikhs can coexist everywhere in the world with a 'personalised' religion, that is 'Sikhism', there is always a grey area of intrusion of some aspects of GurSikhi into the public domain that challenges normative secular laws and public policy. France is a good example of this. There, Sikhs live a life of compromises where they feel they cannot fully manifest their belief as equal citizens, so they forego certain privileges that other citizens have, such as jobs in the State sector. But Sikhs cannot be in a situation of compromises throughout the world. There needs to be some place where 'GurSikhi' as opposed to 'Sikhism' can thrive unobstructed by secular or theological restrictions.

GurSikhi needs to have an independent space for itself so that it can be safe from the prerogatives of State conformism as well as avoid perpetual tension with established systems. This independent space need not be a territorial reality in the form of a separate larger nation

State. It can even be an institution where the remit of a secular or a theological State would end with appropriate arrangements, and extra territorial arrangements.

THE IDEA OF A SIKH STATE

The idea of a Sovereign Sikh State has come up several times particularly since 1945 when the first serious book was published on the need for a Sikh State in the aftermath of decolonisation. Titled 'the idea of the Sikh State', the two authors, Gurbachan Singh and Lal Singh Gyani argued for a 'secular' Sikh State. The idea holds strong appeal since the Sikhs did have a State between 1799 and 1846. It was ruled by a Maharaja. Conscious of the rebellious nature of Sikhs towards authoritarian and hereditary rulers, Maharaja Ranjit Singh cautiously called his Kingdom 'Sarkar- e -Khalsa' rather than Kingdom of Maharaja Ranjit Singh. Sarkar- e - Khalsa means government of the Khalsa. While he had run down the Sarbat Khalsa, he maintained many other aspects of Sikh rule. Sri Akal Takht Sahib nevertheless had its own army under a Jathedar but it was under call of the Government (Maharaja Ranjit Singh). As a ruler, he could theoretically have almost absolute powers but was careful to build consensus. He was able to appoint Hindus and Muslims to powerful positions. He also gave funds to religious institutions of all the religions in his Kingdom to build or maintain mandirs (Hindu temples), mosques, etc. His rule genuinely pursued plurality. His advantage was that he was not subject to democratic compulsion of any dominant or majority pressure group. Hence there was the option for him either to succumb to narrow favouritism towards the Sikh community or as he chose, to be inclusive of all communities in the Kingdom.

The propagators of the Sikh State often cite the rule of Maharaja Ranjit Singh as an example of what a Sikh State would be like. There are in fact differences and contradictions which make that reference irrelevant. The intended Sikh State is presented as a democratic state with modern human rights. This theoretical idea of Sikh State does not explain how a democratic system will stop one dominant community imposing its will on others and excluding them. According to many Sikhs, this has allegedly happened in India where the dominant Hindu community has imposed its cultural outlook over minorities like the Sikhs. There is no reason why something similar will not happen in a democratic Sikh State where a dominant Sikh community may seek to impose its will on minorities such as Hindus.

Moreover, a democratic 'Sikh' State will mean that Sikhs will take up all the powerful positions of decision making. This has its own contradictions in a philosophy which is pluralistic and stresses co-existence. The Sikhs daily pray for the welfare of all humanity and have a proud history of fighting for freedom of conscience and a life of dignity for members of other religious communities and belief systems. A Sikh State in the form of a modern western State would relegate non-Sikhs to reduced rights or survive by forcing large numbers of them out so that they become a minority without the power to control the State or its policies. In other words, the Sikhs would have to be in a significant majority so that even a block vote of non-Sikh minority could not hold the balance of power in the Sikh State. This is contrary to GurSikhi and strikes most Sikhs as undesirable. Brought up to respect every human being and the dignity as well as rights of all, the majority of Sikh people simply do not have the desire to compromise the most fundamental principles of Sikh teachings in favour of a Sikh State. There has not been a political theory of Statecraft developed by

Sikhs that is consistent with the principles of GurSikhi. As a result, there continues to be ambivalence in most Sikhs to the idea of a Sikh State.

Some Sikhs have proposed and sought autonomous status for a Sikh majority state (province) within Indian federation. The autonomous state would be part of the Indian federation, share defence, communications, finances and foreign policy. The idea behind an autonomous Punjab is that it would restrict the scope of the central Government from perpetually interfering politically in the province and further enable the State to develop economically. But the Indian State and its executive is extremely paranoid about decentralising power to the regional States let alone grant them autonomy. The central Government fears that autonomy would lead to separation of the Punjab State from the Union of India and this would start a domino effect around the country, subsequently leading to disintegration of the Indian State. They accuse movements for autonomy of being a prelude to secession. It is an irrational response from the central Government. However central political institutions including the bureaucracy have instinctive centralising tendencies. They were formed under British colonialism and have failed yet to readjust to new realities. They feel threatened when devolution of power campaigns become popular.

A STATE ON SIKH CONCEPTS

The alternative to a nationalist Sikh State in the form of a State dominated by a single ethnic national majority is a State based on concepts and values of GurSikhi. Would such a state be any different than contemporary secular democratic States? Others ask whether it will turn out to be like some of the theocratic States in the Middle East. The answer lies in the distinctive concepts of GurSikhi and their relationship to State theory.

A few aspects of GurSikhi that are often missed are that it emerged at around the same time that Europe was going through tremendous intellectual, social and political upheavals. The regime of absolute Monarchy and Church dominance was being challenged. This resulted in the twentieth century liberal secular democratic State.

GurSikhi too, challenged some of the accepted norms of the time. It uprooted the centuries old hierarchical and divisive system of traditional culture generally called Hinduism, by challenging the notion of Varna-Jaati and gender hierarchy. It also challenged Abrahamic exclusivity. Freedom of conscience and dignity of the human was one of the most important changes that GurSikhi embarked upon. Many of the Sikh battles have been for these two principles.

The dignity of the human led to a number of radical departures from traditional Indian society. It destroyed preferential treatment. Thus everyone was put on an equal footing. Gender discrimination or hierarchy became meaningless. Differences were acknowledged but were not to be the basis of discriminatory practices or hierarchy. Caste was not recognised.

The concept of dignity further led to decision by consensus rather than order by a supreme leader, monarch or spiritual master. After the ten Gurus the Sikhs were to take guidance from Sri Guru Granth Sahib and decide their temporal affairs by consensus of Guru Panth.

Democratic institution within Sikhs was rooted in the process of near unanimous consensus rather than majoritarian verdict. The institution of the Sarbat Khalsa was introduced whereby any Sikh could participate in the decision making. A form of republican system emerged. The democratic system was one that sought widest consensus. Therefore, a State based on Sikh concepts would adopt either a proportional representative type of democracy with weighted representation for minorities in some spheres, particularly where laws could affect them or it would have a power sharing system with elected representatives.

GurSikhi teaches that society is to collectively take care of those who are unfortunate and not defer cause to 'karma'. In most Gurdwaras, food as langar and temporary shelter was and continues to be provided. There were hospitals and places to look after people with severe disabilities.

One fundamental continuity that GurSikhi kept with Indian civilisation was pluralism in the public sphere. Faith and secular ideologies were both coexistent in the public sphere without marginalising one to the personal domain. This is one of the great differences with western State theory. GurSikhi did not eradicate the spiritual, the divine or God from the public sphere but managed to retain it intrinsic to governance without the problems that Europe had. But the different belief systems and their moral codes were all to be respected by the State as long as they did not infringe basic principles of dignity. Hence sati, that is widow burning, was banned. But other practices were accommodated, such as burka for women of other faiths (both Muslims and Hindus), even though GurSikhi does not agree with it.

These complex and progressive set of principles constitute some of the basics of 'Halimi Raj', a theory of Statecraft based on GurSikhi. This is merely a brief overview of a complex political theory. With these principles a State based on Sikh concepts would be remarkably different than an average western secular State. 'Dharam' would not be hidden away or pushed out of the general ethical and other value systems of the State.

While a State based on Sikh concepts would be an expression of GurSikhi in the real world of politics and social sphere, such a State does not fulfil the needs and coordinating role that a worldwide Sikh community needs. Moreover any State, whether a Sikh State or a State based on Sikh value systems, is going to be obsessed with its internal politics rather than be catering for the Global Sikh community. Lastly, as a theory of a Sikh political thought has not yet developed, the idea of a State based on concepts of GurSikhi is a distant proposition.

NON-TERRITORIALITY

Within GurSikhi the spiritual and temporal are integrated and its particular world view is based on the teachings of Sri Guru Granth Sahib. This binds Sikhs across the world as a People. The Sikhs as a People or community call themselves a Qaum, loosely meaning a Nation. But unlike other nations, the concept of Sikh Qaum, also called Panth at times, in a somewhat creative homonym of the later word, is not territorially dependent. It has an inherent logic to survive and function as a non-territorial nation. In fact, the 'Qaum' in Sikhs is essentially a nonterritorial concept that crosses Kingdoms, Empires and nation states as well as borders and continents.

This does not negate a territorially defined nation-state for those Sikhs in a particular part of the world who seek one in that region. But a 'Sikh' territorial statehood can only be based on the Sikh concept of pluralistic political theory rather than a state just for Sikhs or rule just by Sikhs. Even if a pluralistic Sikh State were to emerge, as it did under Maharaja Ranjit Singh, the wider Qaum, or the non-territorial Sikh nation would still exist independently as a larger and more powerful and distinct idea. Such a non-territorial nation is inclusive of Sikhs across the world incorporating those within a probable GurSikhi based State territory and those outside it. In other words, the membership of the 'Qaum' is bigger than a probable territorially limited Sikh State citizenship.

This is a dimension of Sikhdom that has not been properly articulated or proposed in any of the recent struggles of Sikhs nor has it been properly explored. The larger Panth or non-territorial Sikh nation exists irrespective of what arrangements Sikhs make in South Asia, or more specifically in India. The Panth is guided by Sri Guru Granth Sahib.

The non-territorial nation is a unique Sikh concept. The nation is considered to be a European idea although the word nation exists in relation to the Jews and other tribes in the Bible long before the word was coined in modern European history. However, the nation-state as a European idea is considered to have started after the Westphalia treaty of 1648 and subsequently took on greater impetus after the French revolution. It dominates conventional world political thinking.

As a conventional term and operative idea in the contemporary world, people who consider themselves as a nation are either seeking a State, are defined by their territorial concentration and seeking an autonomous region within a country or already have one or the other of the two. Thus the French have a nation state. The Scottish are a substate or autonomous state within the United Kingdom, the Kurds are seeking a State and the Tibetans are allegedly seeking an autonomous State within China. The nation as a phenomenon in the conventional world is therefore tied with territory, defined by territory and either controlling or seeking to control a territory.

Most modern States however do not constitute a single nation of people. Most States have multiple nations within them as India has, even though it denies them that recognition. Switzerland has at least four nations and has recognised them by having four different State languages. The United Kingdom has at least four recognised nations as well. But nations within countries continue to be territorial in nature. Where struggles exist between the country and the nation of people, it almost always concerns territory.

QAUM

The Sikh concept of Qaum evolved as a de-territorialised notion instead of a territorialised concept. During the period of the tenth Guru, Sikhs lived in Sindh, in the Deccan, in Punjab and in several other areas of India. They acted as a people bonded by a language, a scripture, a philosophy and a unique way of organising their community life. The Gurdwara was and remains the focus of the Sikh community in any locality. Although the people from different regions had different mother tongues, the language of Sri Guru Granth Sahib bound them into a community with a single common language.

The Sikhs were to accept Sri Guru Granth Sahib as their guide, Sri Harmandir Sahib as the place where Sri Guru Granth Sahib led the Sikhs in 'raag' and common prayer and Sri Akal Takht Sahib as the institution where Sikhs came together for social, political and religious decisions in consensus. This continues to date. Territory was important to the regional broader community of Sikhs and non-Sikhs but it was not the defining institutionalising aspect for the Sikh community either locally or as a whole. The wider Sikh community came to be known as a Qaum.

The Sikhs as a Qaum evolved over the period of the ten Gurus and their different aspects were consolidated and codified as well as institutionalised by the tenth Guru, Guru Gobind Singh Ji. The features that stand out and made it a Qaum include: an egalitarian community, a system of consensus decision making, an identity, a guiding text or philosophy, a common language, a common code of conduct, a flag, an internal system of justice, resolving disputes, dealing with offenders and a willingness to defend the principles that drive the community.

Over the lives of the ten Gurus, the Sikhs developed the institution of Gurdwara as a common community centre around the Guru Granth

Sahib. The language of the Guru Granth Sahib is also new and unique to Sikhs everywhere. Outside every Gurdwara stands a flagpole displaying the Sikh flag, the Nishan Sahib. The Gurdwara is considered to be the territory of the Sikhs coming together as Panth with the Guru Granth as 'Granth' making the local community mobile, local as well as integrated into the wider Sikh Panth through common features and practices. Thus the Qaum is global and local as a diffuse nation spread across territories.

The only territorial aspect of the 'Qaum' is the local Gurdwara which Sikhs consider as their local autonomous territory and defend it as such, and the central institutions such as Sri Darbar Sahib, which they consider to be common but independent territory of the Global Sikh community. Otherwise the community is dispersed territorially both in the locality and the wider region or even the world, networking globally and locally. The 'Qaum' is therefore de-territorialised for all intent and purpose. If a section of the community moves to another region, as a 'Qaum' it will establish a Gurdwara there and those left in the original locality will carry on. Sometimes nearly the whole community moves. This has happened to several small Sikh communities, such as the ones who moved from small towns of East Africa to India or Europe. The only territorial claim made by the collective community in a locality is the local Gurdwara. The community is politically, socially and philosophically autonomous amidst other people and yet integrated in the wider world without barriers.

This set of factors and this autonomy effectively makes the Sikhs a nation in a global context. It is a nation whose existence, survival and self-definition is not dependent on a large territory as State. The word nation is almost always associated with territory. It may be convenient to introduce the word 'Qaum' to mean a 'Peoples' whose existence and cohesion is de-territorialised by design rather than by political circumstances. In other words, not to use the word 'nation' in context of the organisation of the Sikhs as a 'Peoples'. In that aspect the Sikh Qaum took a different course than the nation in western political theory. As suggested before, the word Sikhs use to define themselves collectively is Qaum. The Qaum comprises highly spiritual individuals as well as those whose faith in metaphysical ideas is agnostic at best. The Qaum is inclusive of those who congregate at the Gurdwara daily and even those who only attend it on special occasions. The Qaum incorporates members who commit to all the ideals and practices endowed to the Sikhs by the Gurus to those who adopt practices selectively.

Although the word 'Qaum' comes from Arabic roots with a slightly different meaning, the word has come to mean the equivalent of 'nation' in the Sikh understanding when used in relation to themselves. It is perhaps a homonym. There is nothing uncommon about this. Many words come from a different language and take on a different meaning in the language in which they are adopted. Perhaps the word curry is the most obvious one. In Indian languages it refers to a particular dish. Imported into the English language, it describes all types of spicy Indian dishes. Hence when the word Qaum is used in relation to the Sikhs it means a non-territorialised 'People'.

Although the Sikhs of Punjab went on to form a territorial Kingdom, two features stand out. Many Sikhs, including some Maharajas remained outside this Kingdom but still saw Sri Akal Takht Sahib and the wider Panth as their nation. Secondly, the Kingdom was run along Sikh principles and was ruled by Sikhs but had people from different cultures and religions. In fact, the Sikhs were a minority. Many powerful positions within the Government of the Sikh Kingdom were occupied by non-Sikhs. It was not a Sikh nation State in the sense of European nation States. In the European State, the dominant group is the nation of people who claim and rule over that land. At best

Maharaja Ranjit Singh's Kingdom could be called a Sikh State but not a Sikh nation State particularly as Sikhs were not confined to that one territory nor did they form the majority and even within the Kingdom they were a minority.

This needs to be understood to appreciate the different concept of the 'Qaum' in Sikhi. The Sikhs who were outside this Kingdom were not a 'diaspora' nor were they pockets of Sikhs left outside the Kingdom or migrants from the Kingdom. In fact, there were at least two small Kingdoms ruled by Sikh rulers, namely Patiala and Kapurthalla, outside the main Sikh Kingdom of Ranjit Singh. Moreover, there were Sikhs in many other parts of India as vibrant communities. But all saw themselves as part of the wider Qaum.

The non-territorial aspect of the Sikhs as a 'Qaum' is consistent with Sri Guru Granth Sahib which repeatedly stresses that attachment to property, land and exclusiveness is antithetical to realising the eternal truth. Therefore, whereas individuals and small groups may place a great deal of importance to territory as possession, the wider Sikh 'Qaum' does not see its survival as a 'Qaum' only if it has permanent possession of land. It is a form of trans-territorial nation which defines itself by a particular belief, language and shared history and is global in nature.

The idea of Qaum does not threaten the territorialised 'Nation State'. It becomes complimentary by finding adjustments to the State in almost every situation.

IS THERE A SIKH DIASPORA?

The Sikh Qaum is a non-territorial concept or rather a trans-territorial concept of the 'nation'. In the modern world, the Sikh Qaum or nation is spread across the globe, thinks in terms of a nation but functions without the necessity of a permanent territory to define its common bond. In the conventional world of globalisation where territorial boundaries have become increasingly porous and the nation as defined by a State is losing its meaning, the Sikhs are well placed for the future world where many nations will attempt to define themselves in terms other than territorial boundary or concentration. It is interesting that the Sikhs are instituted in a way that places them ahead of the trend that the world is moving towards.

From this perspective it is inappropriate to call the Sikhs across the world as a diaspora community. There can be a Punjabi Sikh diaspora but as Sikhs have always constituted several communities and as a 'People' have had no single territorial belonging, the modern Sikh demography across the world is consistent with the original non-territorial community. Today the Sikh Qaum is a global community whereas in the seventeenth century it was a community spread across South Asia. If the Sikhs in the west are a diaspora community today, then the question is who were the Sikhs in Sindh or the Deccan in seventeenth century? Were they also diaspora? Where is the modern Sikh diaspora, diasporic in relation to where? Is it Indian Punjab, Pakistan Punjab, Delhi, Sindh, Deccan or Peshawar? And what about the third or fourth generation Sikhs in Britain, Canada or America? At best the first generation can be diasporic in reference to South Asia, but South Asia has never been a homogenous united region. It is the equivalent of saying a Scot in Africa is diasporic from Europe! The word does not make much sense when used in relation to Sikhs worldwide. There is no Sikh diaspora.

COMPLICATIONS OF NON-TERRITORIALITY

Non-territoriality leads to a different form of conflict. For guidance to be independent of any secular or other similar constraints or from influence from other theological powers, the interpretation of Sri Guru Granth Sahib for the collective decision of the Panth on any particular issue has to be in an independent environment where only the remit of Sri Guru Granth Sahib is exercised. In other words, the political reality of the place where Sikhs gather to make decisions has to be independent of other sovereignties and autonomous in its own right where there is absolute supremacy of the Guru without any political or legal shadow over it.

As has been argued throughout this book, this is not possible under the current constitutional order in any country of the world. Every country has its own distinctive form of sovereignty. While in some countries, the constitution and laws of the country would not be contrary to or be threatened by most interpretations of Sri Guru Granth Sahib, in others, constitutional restrictions on rights and freedoms may interfere with an independent discussion and decisions based on Sri Guru Granth Sahib. Moreover, as has been experienced repeatedly in India, the decision-making process of the Panth is often sabotaged or interfered with by political parties in the wider political arena for their own prerogatives.

The modern nation state is an institution that has the capacity to interfere in and impose its remit upon every individual and every institution within its territory by virtue of appropriating legitimate violence solely into its own hands. Unlike Mughal times when Sikhs could gather out of the Mughal reach and avoid restrictive environments, no such possibility is now realistic except by arrangement in the modern world. This limits the scope of the Sikh Panth to decide its options freely.

For instance, the Panth may decide differential approaches in different countries to a specific issue depending on local politics, language and concepts, but even to do so, the discussion leading to such particular stances have to be made in an independent environment and not under the constraints and restrictive scope of the country. These compromises still have to be consistent with general principles of GurSikhi, or considered as temporary derogations until that country is willing to accommodate the complexities. France is again an example in mind, where the state interprets 'secularity' rather rigidly while Sikhs do not think wearing the turban challenges secularity.

Consequently, a contradiction emerges. While a State just for Sikhs without parity of citizenship for non-Sikhs is against Sikh principles, for the Sikhs to make decisions based on Guru Granth Sahib, independent of any external influence, there has to be some form of autonomous Sikh territory where the jurisdiction of any other State system does not extend or impose. The Sikhs have to have a free and independent space to decide their affairs.

This is one of the dilemmas that faces the Sikhs at the moment. All Gurdwaras are subject to the jurisdiction of the country they are in, thus making any self-assumed supremacy of Guru Granth-Guru Panth subservient to that of the State in reality. In other words, the supremacy of Guru Granth Sahib can only be in the minds of the Sikhs but not in the real world of engagement because the laws of the State can restrict the Guru Granth Sahib's interpretation into practice.

There is no place or institution in the world where the worldwide Panth representatives can gather independently in a self-juristic Sikh environment. It is a problem that has emerged as a result of the modern reality of State system and division of the entire earth into the control of different sovereignties.

CHANGED DEMOGRAPHY OF THE PANTH

About sixty years ago a significant majority of the Sikh Panth, almost 80% if not more, lived in the Punjab. Migrations and territorial changes have changed that. Almost 40% Sikhs now live outside Punjab and of these some 20% live outside India.

This changed demography and the reality of the nation state in the modern world calls for a new strategy for Sikhs to continue to be guided independently by the Guru Granth Sahib in spiritual and temporal affairs and for such guidance to be directed in the form of institutional decision making as laid out by the Gurus.

Within GurSikhi, the anarchy of individual interpretation is limited. The Panth is encouraged to collectively decide on interpretation. The proposition that every individual Sikh can make his or her own decision irrespective of community is inconsistent with the Sarbat Khalsa concept.

A major problem faced by Sikhs is that they are at the mercy of their State's help when dealing with issues around the world. They have to request States, including India, to take up the issue on their behalf. There is no direct representation of the Sikhs at any international platform independent of the countries of residence or other Non-Government Organisations.

This is a major handicap. The Sikhs are unable to educate the world or interact at the United Nations, independently of India, UK or Canada, the three main countries where they have significant populations. Nor can they independently make decisions outside the jurisdictions of the States they are in.

Moreover, there is no recognisable body of Sikhs, let alone an international one, that can claim to represent the Sikhs or have in place a process for national let alone international consensus on a particular issue.

At this time in history, there is considerable fragmentation and individualism which is partly due to lack of coherent or representative bodies and lack of space in which to make their decisions.

Since neither a Sikh State is a viable option in a period of 'equal opportunity' for all nor is there a theory of a State based on Sikh principles, perhaps the one institution and area that can be independent is the Darbar Sahib and Sri Akal Takht sahib.

THE PROPOSAL

- THE CENTRAL INSTITUTION
- SRI DARBAR SAHIB
- FUNCTIONAL AND ARCHITECTURAL PRINCIPLES OF SRI DARBAR SAHIB COMPLEX
    - SRI HARMANDAR SAHIB
    - SRI AKAL TAKHT SAHIB
- ANOINTING JATHEDAR SRI AKAL TAKHT SAHIB
- CONFLICT OF SOVEREIGNTIES
- SUPREMACY OF SRI AKAL TAKHT SAHIB
- EXTRA TERRITORIAL ARRANGEMENT
- LIMITATIONS OF SHIROMANI GURDWARA PARBHANDIK COMMITTEE
- ANTER RASHTRY GURDWARA SABHA (ASGS)
- SETTING UP THE ASGS
- BUNGHE
- INTERNATIONAL ENGAGEMENT
- FULL MEMBERSHIP
- OBSERVER STATUS
- NGO STATUS
- INTERNATIONAL ENGAGEMENT OPTIONS
- ADVANTAGES TO SIKHS
- ADVANTAGES TO PUNJAB
- ADVANTAGES TO INDIA
- ADVANTAGES TO SOUTH ASIA

THE CENTRAL INSTITUTION

Sri Akal Takht Sahib within Sri Darbar Sahib offers the option of being an independent central institution that networks with Sikhs all over the world, represents their interests and brings them together when major decisions are to be made. This would then be consistent with the non-territorial identity of the Sikh as a 'People'.

Sri Akal Takht Sahib as a centralising institution and Sri Harmandir Sahib in Sri Darbar Sahib complex can become the global focal place with no legal jurisdiction or political control over it other than by the Global Sikh community. A networking structure would be an international organisation that coordinates activities.

SRI DARBAR SAHIB

Sri Darbar Sahib is a unique institution. Apart from its architectural splendour and the magnificence of Sri Harmandir Sahib, its entire structural construction is designed to signify and ensure certain Sikh principles.

In the Sikh Panth all the Sikh Gurus made great efforts to stop idolatry, personality cult and dependency. Repeatedly they reminded the Sikhs that while they, the Gurus, were their guides; they were in fact no more than guides to a higher reality. Their message always was for people to become self-sufficient, self-aware and self-confident in themselves. Thus they discouraged cultish behaviour towards themselves. They also refused to become living idols or be portrayed and revered as stone idols after their departure. They encouraged Sikhs to stand on their own feet and believe in themselves as a community.

The third Guru, Guru Amardas, acquired land and started to build a site for the Sikhs, called Amritsar. The fifth Guru consolidated these efforts and finished constructing Sri Harmandir Sahib, which later was Gold leafed, in the middle of a water pool.

What is significant about this place is that it is not the birth place of the first Sikh Guru, Guru Nanak. The birth place is Nankana Sahib. The second Guru onward did not choose Nankana Sahib as the common place of the Sikhs. Instead they chose Amritsar, about 100 km from Nankana Sahib itself.

The sixth Guru introduced another institution in the complex which is innovative in South Asian history. This is called Sri Akal Takht Sahib. It has variably been called Thara Sahib and Akal Bunga in history. The Akal Takht was enacted as a place of temporal sovereignty of the Sikhs. Sri Akal Takht Sahib is the embodiment of the non-territorial nation represented through its institution. Here the Guru sat in audience as Regal, and passed edicts for the Sikhs in their spiritual and temporal issues. Here wars were declared and an Army was maintained.

In the lives and works of the subsequent Gurus, both Sri Harmandir Sahib and Sri Akal Takht Sahib were maintained but the Gurus did not institutionally use the Takht Sahib. Perhaps one of the reasons was that while there were living Gurus, the need for a sovereign institution independent of the Gurus did not make sense. However, the infrastructure and principles were retained.

FUNCTIONAL AND ARCHITECTURAL PRINCIPLES OF SRI DARBAR SAHIB COMPLEX

The institutions in Sri Darbar Sahib bring to life many aspects of the Sikh teachings. The complex as a whole is called Darbar Sahib. In it the two important institutions are Sri Harmandir Sahib and Sri Akal Takht Sahib.

SRI HARMANDIR SAHIB

Sri Harmandir Sahib is a place where only the word of the Gurus is spoken or recited. No one makes speeches or sermons. This is where the Guru Granth Sahib is brought physically every day. The Granth Sahib is recited in the 'raags'.

In many texts it has been suggested that Sri Harmandir Sahib is the spiritual place in the complex where the praises of God are sung and nothing else. However, it is the Guru Granth Sahib that is recited. The Guru Granth Sahib is not just praising of the eternal. It incorporates political philosophy, a philosophy of ethics and many other aspects of human life. Perhaps it is correct to say that Sri Harmandir Sahib is where only the Guru Granth Sahib speaks in person as Guru, through others. It is perhaps not so much 'worshipping' as the Shabad Guru in spoken form.

The Harmandir Sahib is where the Guru sits and speaks. The daily practices of set recitations take place in the mornings, evenings and late evenings after which the Guru departs for the night. In between, Raagis (singers) sing verses from Guru Granth Sahib. The Guru Granth Sahib is ceremoniously taken to Sri Akal Takht Sahib for the night. Early next morning the Guru Granth Sahib is ceremoniously brought to Sri Harmandir Sahib.

Opposite is the Sri Akal Takht Sahib, whose doors do not directly face Sri Harmandir Sahib. Sri Akal Takht Sahib is where the Panth, or the Sikhs as a collective, gather to make important interpretations and decisions based on the teachings of the Gurus, i.e. the Guru Granth Sahib.

The Akal Takht signifies the Sikh concept of the living Guru, Guru Granth and Guru Panth. The tenth Guru stated that the Guru is alive in a body of Sikhs particularly when there are at least five Amritdhari Sikhs working together for a consensus decision or action.

Therefore, the Harmandir Sahib is where the Guru Granth Sahib sits for all of humankind. Here every person is welcome irrespective of religion, background or birth. The person is in essence listening to the Guru and joining in praises of the eternal as well as listening to the philosophy of the Guru. This is an individual act of the person. How much an individual listens to or accepts is entirely his or her personal choice. But it is incumbent upon Sikhs to ensure that the Shabad Guru, Sri Guru Granth Sahib, as recited is accessible to anyone without restrictions. The reciting, the management of the place and ensuring its access is conducted entirely by Sikhs who are Amritdharis.

In the Akal Takht Sahib is the seat where those who have made a solemn commitment to the Guru's teachings, i.e., the Amritdhari Sikhs, come together and deliberate according to their understanding of the Guru. It is the belief of Sikhs that the word of the Guru, i.e., the Guru Granth Sahib, is inviolable and uncontestable. However, it is in interpretation that mistakes and misunderstandings arise due to human fallibility.

If the complex is taken into context, it signifies the non-dual philosophy of GurSikhi. GurSikhi does not divide the spiritual from the temporal. In the Darbar Sahib complex as a whole, the spiritual and the temporal come together to form one union, thus the complex completes the concept and puts it into practice. It starts from the listening stage to imparting power of decision and action in the believers.

The Harmandir Sahib is where the philosophy of Miri Piri is revealed daily while the Akal Takht Sahib is where action is taken based on interpretations of this philosophy. Consequently, it is consistent to suggest that Sri Harmandir Sahib is the place of eternal guidance and Sri Akal Takht Sahib is the temporal institution of giving form to this guidance. Both have the same non-dualist approach. One is where the message is while the other is where the message is translated into action.

The Darbar Sahib is therefore GurSikhi in practice in all essence. It is meant to be the common place of all Sikhs where Sikhs from across the world come together. Each aspect of it is designed to reflect Sikh principles. The water signifies the importance of water to evolution of life. The Harmandir Sahib has four doors welcoming everyone irrespective of birth, background and place of origin.

The Akal Takht Sahib is the supreme temporal seat of Sikhs where the committed gather to interpret guidance and then make collective decisions on common issues arising out of their interactions in the everyday world.

The Darbar Sahib as a complex cannot have any jurisdiction other than of the Guru in the place. Other jurisdictions bring the Darbar Sahib complex immediately into a theoretical if not real conflict of autonomy and supremacy.

Influenced by the dualist language of the modern world that divides religion from secular, many Sikhs have increasingly treated the Darbar Sahib as a place of worship. Consequently, its relevance to sustaining and developing GurSikhi as a worldview and the Sikh Panth as a Qaum is becoming marginal as well as ineffective. The Sikhs are increasingly turning into worshippers rather than as doers or as a nation with its own outlook and philosophy which can contribute to the problems of our world.

SRI AKAL TAKHT SAHIB

Sri Akal Takht was built to assert the independent status of the Sikhs and GurSikhi. It is where the interpretation of the Guru's message is given practical expression. Built by Sri Guru Hargobind Sahib, the sixth Guru, its (Sri Akal Takht Sahib's) first act, according to Sikh historians, was to request Sikhs to bring arms and horses to the Takht. A standing army was set up. It became clear that GurSikhi was not a personal faith or just a set of practices for worshipping, but a living philosophy that set out to make an impact in the world, protect itself and physically be a presence.

Sri Akal Takht has had a variable history. During the time of the Gurus, it was unnecessary to continue to treat it as a place of sovereignty where the Guru must sit. During the earthly life of the Gurus, the Guru was supreme and with his Sikhs the sovereignty was complete. The significance of Sri Akal Takht Sahib took practical form after Guru Gobind Singh ji when the Guruship was passed to Sri Guru Granth Sahib and Guru Panth.

Although the Guru Granth and Guru Panth, wherever the two are together, become sovereign, the institutionalisation of this supremacy in a particular site makes it both significant, institutionalised and real.

Thus, in theory, the Sikh Panth is meant to gather and make announcements of its collective decisions at Sri Akal Takht Sahib. There then follow commitments by Sikhs, albeit voluntarily, to such collective decisions. By having a central institution and a process, it enables a decision to have authority and respect. If decisions are made sporadically anywhere wherever there are a few Sikhs, this could cause chaos and conflicting decisions. While the practice of meeting in a place other than Sri Akal Takht Sahib is possible in principle, it has to have the common consent of the entire or significant Panth. For instance, during a war, or other crises when Darbar Sahib was not easily accessible to the Sikhs, the Sikh Panth gathered elsewhere as Guru Granth-Guru Panth.

The gathering of Sikhs for the purpose of collective decision is called Sarbat Khalsa. At each gathering the Sarbat Khalsa decided on a leader, or rather a coordinator or spokesperson. This eventually became institutionalised.

During Maharaja Ranjit Singh's Kingdom, the Sarbat Khalsa was held in the early years of his reign. However, feeling threatened by a parallel seat of authority in his Kingdom, he closed down the Sarbat Khalsa. He could not marginalise Sri Akal Takht Sahib. In fact, he honoured it either due to pragmatic reasons or inspired by reverence. He treated it more sovereign than himself, particularly in matters of ethics.

The Takht suffered interference after the fall of the Sikh Kingdom and the imposition of the British raj. The British attempted to control the leadership of the Takht in the Panth and insisted on appointing a custodian calling him the Sabrah. The Sabrah had some form of permanency until another was appointed. However, the Takht's independence from British interference was restored in 1920 in some form and institutionalised to comply with modern institutional systems. The office of Sabrah was brought to an end and the office of Jathedar instituted. The Sikhs rightly described Sri Akal Takht Sahib as a place of spiritual and temporal supremacy of Sikhs. The Jathedar was in essence a spokesperson of the Sikhs and the person who developed consensus.

ANNOINTING JATHEDAR SRI AKAL TAKHT SAHIB

The Jathedar is not the same as the Pope who has divine authority. The divine authority of the Jathedar is in fact the divinity of the Panth and the Jathedar acting with consensus for the Panth.

It is important for the Jathedar to develop and work with consensus before making a decision. Currently the final decisions are made by five

Jathedars. The other four Jathedars belong to four other Takhts. But it is Sri Akal Takht Sahib that is supreme.

It was tradition since 1925 to appoint the Jathedar with the consent of the Sikh Panth. The process was executed with the help of the SGPC as it was and still is the largest Sikh body. The SGPC assumed responsibility for the management of Darbar Sahib, following an Act enacted by the British, the 1925 Gurdwara Act. In the matter of the Jathedar, SGPC took soundings from various Sikh institutions and proposed a few non-controversial nominee. It then consulted the main bodies of the Sikhs, such as the Damdami Taksal, the Deras, the Chief Khalsa Dewan, the Akhand Kirtani Jatha and so on. Following the consultations, the person who commanded almost unanimous respect from the Sikhs was anointed Jathedar.

This system has now broken down as the SGPC has assumed sole responsibility and abandoned consultations. It has started to appoint Jathedars without holding wide consultation. The legal authority of the SGPC to do this is contestable.

There have been proposals for the Jathedar to have a term contract with a wage, retirement package and 'rights' of employment. There are others who find this inconsistent with the Office of the Jathedar. A term contract and rights of employment makes the Jathedar an employee rather than the 'Jathedar' or head of the worldwide Sikhs. It also puts the Jathedar in a subservient role to the body that pays for the wage, retirement and monitors the 'contract'. It takes away the independence of the office.

One of the proposals that has been floated is that the Sri Akal Takht Sahib have its own administration independent of any one body, has its own financial management system and be accountable to the collective of organisations, Sampardas and Sikh institutions. A Board drawn from many institutions around the world could be set up.

The Jathedar has to be selected and appointed by the Sarbat Khalsa. The institution of Sarbat Khalsa needs a lot of thinking and planning in the conventional world as Sikhs are spread all over the world. However, a system can be developed with the help of thinkers, IT experts, administrators and Sikh Sampardas that is fair and inclusive of all schools of thought through their representatives.

CONFLICT OF SOVEREIGNTIES

However, there is an important issue concerning Sri Akal Takht Sahib. As an institution that is self-sovereign, it cannot accept or have the jurisdiction of any authority, other than that of Guru Granth and the Sikh Panth. It is supreme in its own right, representing the seat of sovereignty of Global Sikhs as a people or a Qaum.

This poses a problem in its current status. Sri Akal Takht Sahib is in Indian territory and therefore under Indian jurisdiction. It cannot exercise 'supremacy' or 'self-governance' in reality except in the imagination of the Sikhs. It has however exercised defacto supremacy to some extent. For it to be supreme in real terms, it has to be free of the jurisdiction of any State (including the jurisdiction of a Sikh State, were that to exist). The State has its own prerogatives that are secular and involve interaction in the power games of political groups as well as international partners and international relations. The Takht represents the entire Global Sikh Qaum, not just the Sikhs in the State or regions immediately surrounding the Takht. As a representative institution of the entire Global Panth, the Takht has to be free of the political priorities or ambitions of one regional political group.

Therefore, the Akal Takht needs to be realistically supreme and independent in its own right, free of any legal or political shadow over it and it has to be representative of the entire Panth. It has to establish de jure supremacy recognised in international law and relations.

SUPREMACY OF SRI AKAL TAKHT SAHIB

The supremacy of Sri Akal Takht Sahib, as a coordinating and functioning sovereignty of the institution of Guru Granth-Guru Panth is a proposal that has many benefits to Sikhs, Punjab, India, South Asia and in fact the world. In an independent environment, such as a Darbar Sahib complex without any jurisdiction over it, there is scope to set up institutional systems under Supremacy of Sri Akal Takht Sahib that will develop a Sikh critical perspective on every day and meta policy issues. It will also have the freedom to help form foundations of Sikh ethical and principal concepts.

This proposal could be quite a sensitive issue in India. For a start India will have to cede Darbar Sahib the right to be a distinct and separate territorial institution.

Apart from the politics of it, India has many worries about such action. It could argue that there will be copycat demands. However, there is no other institution with similar history and principle as the Sri Akal Takht Sahib in India. Christianity and Islam have their sovereign institutions elsewhere in the world, namely Vatican (Catholics), UK (through the Queen for Anglicism) and Mecca (Muslims). Buddhists do not have a tradition of institutional sovereignty, but one branch of it accords sovereign status to the living Dalai Lama. Hindus do not have such traditions and in fact it could be argued that a sovereign institution would be contrary to Hindu thought, especially Sanatan Dharma of Hinduism. The Matths are not Takhts. Hinduism diffuses within the State. Judaism has vested its sovereignty in the State of Israel. Jainism does not have an institutional tradition of sovereign political body. Consequently, the status of Sri Akal Takht is unique in South Asia.

The issue of copycat demands does not arise and the Indian State should be able to deal with such demands.

India will further be worried about the Darbar Sahib becoming a possible safe haven for alleged insurgents and political activity against it. If the pattern of the Vatican is followed, then this becomes an obsolete argument. India could enter into extra-territorial arrangements as Italy has with the Vatican.

For instance, the defence of Sri Darbar Sahib could be set up as a non-threatening integrated system within South Asia, particularly India just as the current police escort system for the protection of the Jathedar and SGPC officials. Criminal law could also be deferred to Indian court systems with some modifications. Currency and transport could also be incorporated into the Indian system for convenience.

EXTRA-TERRITORIAL ARRANGEMENT

The Sikhs could make extra-territorial arrangements for Sri Darbar Sahib, in effect for Sri Akal Takht Sahib, with the Indian State. This would meet the worries of the Indian State and enable the Takht to be self-juristic and representative of Sikhs worldwide as the Vatican is for Catholics.

With the support of India, the Akal Takht could be incorporated into the United Nations system as an observer member initially. As relations with India become comfortable and the later is reassured, different arrangements could be considered if needed. However, it will be better if Sri Akal Takht Sahib stays away from the intrigues of international politics and avoid full state membership. An observer status has the best of all worlds.

After the principle is accepted politically by all parties, the question arises, 'What extent of territory would be accorded this extra-territorial status?' This depends on negotiations and what is mutually acceptable to the Sikhs and India. The main issue is an agreement in principle.

The other important question is who would manage it and how would the Global Sikh community participate in its functioning? This question is closely tied to the international representation of Sikhs within the NGO sector. Currently the Shiromani Gurdwara Parbhandik Committee unconstitutionally manages the affairs of Sri Akal Takht Sahib and claims to speak on behalf of the Global Sikh community without that remit.

LIMITATIONS OF SHIROMANI GURDWARA PARBHANDIK COMMITTEE

The Shiromani Gurdwara Parbhandik Committee, SGPC, was set up in 1920 when the Sikh Gurdwara movement started. It was formally instituted and recognised by an act of Government, called the 1925 Gurdwara Act.

The Gurdwara Act was enacted by the British. Its purpose was to recover historic Sikh shrines and Gurdwaras for the community. Many of these had become personal properties of the priests by default when land ownership schemes and laws were introduced in India by the British. The Sikhs campaigned for over 5 years to reverse this ownership and further stop British interference by reclaiming Gurdwaras as common community property rather than the property of an individual.

The Gurdwara Act was introduced when East and West Punjab was one state and included Haryana and parts of Himachal Pradesh all as Punjab. At the time, almost 95% of Sikhs lived in the Punjab.

The SGPC has a body of members chosen by election called by the District Commissioner of Amritsar. The District Commissioner is a civil servant of the Indian Government. He or she can be from any background, religion, ethnicity, etc, as long as the person is a member of the Elite Indian civil service, the Indian Administrative Service.

The SGPC has an executive committee which meets once a month and decides on important issues. The general body only meets twice a year for about four hours each time. There are 183 members in the general body.

The SGPC manages the Darbar Sahib among many other Sikh institutions. It has taken upon itself to appoint the Jathedar although no such power is legally accorded to it.

The SGPC has also been making decisions on Sikh religious affairs. This is a power it has allocated to itself in recent times and it presumes erroneously, that it has legal jurisdiction to decide on Sikh religious matters. It is in fact unconstitutional as the Indian constitution is secular and the State cannot directly or indirectly interfere in a religion except where there is a violation of the law as explained earlier. Since SGPC is a statutory body, it is in fact a State body. By appointing the Jathedar and deciding religious issues, it draws the Indian State into controversial and unconstitutional actions.

The SGPC influences the entire Sikh community on three important issues. However, its mandate does not allow it to represent the entire Sikh community anymore since a substantive number of Sikh community is outside Punjab and India.

1. It manages a common site of the Global Sikh Panth and makes decisions regarding its practices without consulting Sikhs outside its own constituency or representation.

2. It appoints the Jathedar and interferes in Sri Akal Takht Sahib, without consulting Sikh bodies in Punjab let alone Sikhs outside Punjab.

3. It takes religious decisions for the entire Sikh community without having the mandate by the Sikh community worldwide. Moreover, this is unconstitutional.

The SGPC is further hampered by its statutory status. As a State body it cannot represent Sikhs worldwide, particularly Sikhs who are not Indian citizens. Secondly it cannot act as a Non-Government Organisation in International institutions such as the United Nations, the European Union, the World Parliament of Religions etc. The changed Sikh demography now calls for a different body to be able to represent the Sikhs worldwide both in terms of membership and in international forums.

ANTER-RASHTRY SHIROMANI GURDWARA SABHA (ASGS)

It is important for a body to represent as many Sikhs as possible from around the world. A suggested model for this is an Anter-Rashtari (International) Shiromani Gurdwara Sabha with members from Punjab, Delhi, other parts of India, Canada, USA, UK, Europe and other parts of the world.

Such a body could have a membership system proportional to the number of Sikhs in the region or State. For instance, if 70% of Sikhs live in Punjab, the body could have 70% members from Punjab. If 5% live in Delhi, then 5% of the seats in the body could be allocated to Delhi and so on.

The body could then hold wide consultations among general Sikh bodies and its own constituency, before making important decisions. It could become the consulting body in the appointment of the Jathedar. It would represent Sikhs in international institutions.

The body would need to set up national consulting mechanisms in different countries. Such a mechanism will need to have competent people and go through issues carefully before involving the Sri Akal Takht Sahib.

However, the body would only be an NGO as far as the UN is concerned and will not have the status of a State member, particularly as it would be an international body. Sri Akal Takht Sahib on the other hand would have status as a member State. The two would complement each other's work internationally.

It is suggested that such a body be called Antar-rashtry Shiromani Gurdwara Sabha (ASGS) or a similar name.

SETTING UP THE ASGS

Many Sikhs are overwhelmed by the idea of an international Sikh body and wonder whether the fractious politics of Sikhs can enable the formation of such an organisation. In fact, almost all communities in the world have several divisive factions. The Sikhs in fact have relatively smaller number of factions. The ASGS or equivalent is not an insurmountable exercise. It could be achieved in three phases. Initially the major Sikh national bodies could form the ASGS with the provision to extend the membership and change the format of the membership to make it inclusive.

For instance the SGPC, the DSGMC (Delhi Sikh Gurdwara Management Committee) and other Indian statutory Gurdwara bodies such as Nander Sahib Board, along with the Pakistan Gurdwara Parbhandik Committee (PGPC,) the USA ones, called AGPC and WSC-US, the Canadian one, called CGPC and an equivalent in the

UK, as well as national bodies from other countries or the largest
Gurdwara from a country, can all join this body in the first phase. The
number of members needs to be proportional to the Sikh population
in the region. For instance, as SGPC allegedly represents nearly 70%
of the Sikh population, it should have 70% of the seats accorded to it.
The DSGMC apparently represents some 5% of the Sikh population.
It will have 5% seats. And so on. The members can then select or
elect the office bearers for limited terms. The body will have to set up
a secretariat, a constitutional, policy and membership advisory body
which will take it towards phases two and three.

In the second phase, the ASGS needs to develop criteria to make
itself inclusive and representative of other Sikhs and Sikh organisations.
Institutions and organisations that dissent from larger national
organisations, (i.e. if a body in Punjab is in conflict with SGPC, or
simply maintains independent status) will all need to be brought into
some form of membership. The ASGS can also make provision for co-
options of talented and experienced Sikh individuals.

In the third phase, the ASGS will need to make its national bodies
reflect Sikh practises of representation rather than western formats.
This could take considerable time as Sikh scholars have neither paid
any attention to this nor have considered the possibility that there
are different approaches between the two systems. With an inclusive
form of representative membership, the ASGS could become the
institutionalised form of Sarbat Khalsa and the Sarbat Khalsa can be
organised by it under orders of Sri Akal Takht Sahib. However, these
are matters of detail and function which are the prerogative of the
institution and the international body when one is set up.

This will make the role of Sri Akal Takht Sahib a lot easier to
manage since a body (ASGS) to assist with consensus forming will be
in place. The Jathedar will have the role of ensuring Gurmat principles

and develop diplomatic relations in the name of Sri Akal Takht Sahib on behalf of the Sikhs.

BUNGHE

There needs to be reasonable land attached to Sri Darbar Sahib where both offices and residential rest places can be built. Every day in the Ardas (Sikh prayer), Sikhs say 'Bunghe Jugo Jug Atal'. A Bungha is essentially a place of community residence, a place of learning or a form of administrative branch of a group.

Previously Bunghe were built and maintained by different Misls, Gianis (learned scholars who taught Gurbani or Kirtan) or of a group of villages or even an administrative office at Sri Darbar Sahib by a Raja or Maharaja.

As the demography of the Sikhs has changed, the institution of Bunghas also has to adapt. These days they are often called 'Saraan'. A Darbar Sahib that is self-juristic and outside the territorial governance of India, will need to provide land for Sikhs from across the world to have offices and representation to have a meaningful system of assembly. These offices cum residential rest houses can be built by Sikhs of different countries and be called Bunghas. For instance, there can be a British or Walaiti Bungha, an American or Amriki Bungha, a Canadian Bungha or Bungha Canadian wallehian da, etc. There can also be Bunghes of some of the big seminaries. People from these countries can have their own residential resting rooms without always struggling to find a place.

Sri Darbar Sahib and the land around it could become a genuine place of worldwide Sikhs, with their own 'embassies' or representative offices and residences that will engage with Sri Akal Takht Sahib as well as offer a place for meetings and rest when visiting Sri Darbar Sahib.

INTERNATIONAL ENGAGEMENT

Finally coming to the specific question posed by Sardar Gurcharan Singh Tohra. How do the Sikhs get some form of international representation? It is important to explain some institutional arrangements and status in international institutions before making specific suggestions particularly at United Nations.

There are three main possibilities of representation at the United Nations:

- The first is as a full member
- The second is as an observer member
- The third is as an NGO, (non-governmental organisation).

FULL MEMBERSHIP

Full membership is available to States (countries). Full membership entails getting involved in almost all activities of the UN and having voting rights in the General Assembly as well as the committees the country is in. All countries are full members. Switzerland, through its own choice, was not a full member until recently.

OBSERVER STATUS

Observer status is granted to States or States in waiting or some international institutions. Observer Status gives access to almost all bodies of the UN but does not grant voting rights. The Vatican has an observer status and is officially called Holy See. The Observer status keeps it immune from getting embroiled in the intrigues of international politics and voting in unpopular or unethical issues. The Palestine State, although not yet existing as an independent State, also has observer status. There are many inter-governmental institutions such as the Commonwealth, African Union, EU, etc, and several UN associated entities such as International Criminal Court with Observer status.

NGO STATUS

NGO status, which means Non-Governmental Status, does not grant any voting rights nor does it grant any right to speak. Provisions to make statements are given by the UN in many of its bodies to certain categories of NGOs. NGOs however are under the jurisdiction of the country they are located in, and although make independent statements and campaign independently of the prerogatives of the State, they do not have the status that States enjoy.

There are three forms of NGO status:

- **Rooster**
- **Special**
- **General**

INTERNATIONAL ENGAGEMENT OPTIONS

The Sikhs have the following alternative options to engage internationally with countries, international organisations and regional organisations. It is better to acquire both.

STATE MEMBERSHIP

A. Sri Akal Takht Sahib can get member status as a state once its de jure self-governing supremacy is recognised in international relations.

It can make a claim for observer status similar to that of the Vatican, (Holy See as it is officially called). This will absolve it from paying heavy dues and participating or taking sides in highly charged political issues such as the international war. Sri Akal Takht Sahib then will not put the lives of Sikhs anywhere in jeopardy if it stays away from real politick.

This will give the Sikhs an independent role in the UN which is autonomous of the debate concerning a larger and separate Sikh State. It will also allow its representatives to interact with diplomats and governments, thus giving it direct access to take up issues as that of the turban, with the countries concerned.

NGO

The Shiromani Gurdwara Parbhandik Committee cannot directly apply for NGO status. This is because it is a statutory body, therefore linked to the Government. Secondly, it is based in just one region of one country. NGO general status is generally granted to international organisations rather than to those based in one country. Moreover, by definition, an NGO, is a Non-Governmental Organisation, hence cannot be a statutory body.

The Anter Rashtry Shiromani Gurdwara Sabha (ASGS) can apply for general NGO consultative status as a representative NGO of Sikhs across the world. This would place it on par with the World Council of Churches, the Pax Romana, the World Muslim Council, the World Buddhist Council, the Bahais and other cultural and religious based NGOs with consultative status at the United Nations. The ASGS could apply for consultative status immediately after formation.

Currently the Sikh Human Rights Group has ECOSOC special consultative status at the United Nations. However, the organisation does not claim to represent 'Sikhs' as a community or speak for GurSikhi. It is a human rights related body of members.

Rooster membership gives access to some UN conferences and meetings but does not entitle the NGO to make statements except in limited platforms.

Special membership is granted to specialist organisations, such as an organisation of engineers, or airline pilots, etc, or those with wide interest with focus in one or in a few areas, but can still be internationally representative. They can also be organisations representing communities of similar interest. These NGOs are given access to a lot more UN committees and conferences and have the right to speak for limited periods of time (i.e. 1-5 minutes in most cases) in these venues.

General membership This is granted to an organisation with interest in several fields and has international representative character. It has access to almost all committees and conferences, except closed sections of the UN. It also has the provision to speak on almost all platforms, submit papers, etc. The speaking opportunities are however short, between 1-5 minutes.

ADVANTAGES TO SIKHS

By having extra-territorial status, the Darbar Sahib can be free from the internal politics of India and Punjab. It can genuinely be a common place for Sikhs worldwide. It can set up its own Universities and Research and Training institutions that are independent from the constraints of factional, secular, theocratic and other State priorities. And it could sustain the notion of Global Sikh Qaum as a non-territorialised nation.

Extra–territorial status will have another impact on the Punjab. The Akali Dal is a party that perpetually seems to be tied to Sikh religious issues and finds that it has to take these up in its political manifestoes.

The party can be freed to become a constructive participant in Punjab's secular politics. It can take members from all communities without making them feel subservient to Sikh aspirations. Sikhs in other parties can also participate in religious issues without making party political points. Currently most parties in Punjab are tied to and locked with the religious issues of Sikhs, either as supporters or as antagonists.

Extra-territorial status will allow the Akal Takht to develop relations with governments around the world and deal with Sikhs everywhere without having to demand representation of issues by the Indian government or by another Government where Sikhs reside. It will also free the Indian State from being perpetually tested for its support or lack of it for Sikh issues around the world.

An Anter-Rashtry Shiromani Gurdwara Sabha will enable Sikhs across the world to discuss matters on the strength of the rights available to them in their countries. Currently all debate in SGPC has to be cognisant of the Indian Constitution and there is no provision for international representations. The Sikhs will have an international standing in the NGO sector similar to other major faith communities around the world.

ADVANTAGES TO PUNJAB

Extra territorial status for Sri Darbar Sahib will have a significant impact on the politics and economy of Punjab. Since 1947, Punjab has continuously been embroiled in politics of the Sikhs and GurSikhi. Whether it is the Akali Dal which plays up threats to GurSikhi to win over the Sikh electorate or whether it is Congress whose Punjab leader takes up major Sikh projects or issues to solicit Sikh voters, most parties try and appeal to Sikh 'religious' sentiments. Even AAP (Aam Aadmi

Party), the new entrant in Punjab politics, has tried to exploit Sikh issues dating from the 1984 attack on Sri Darbar Sahib.

The effect of this form of politics is that it communalises the political arena. Minority communities in Punjab feel marginalised, sometimes isolated and sometimes demonised. This particularly has an effect on the Punjabi Hindus. A perpetual fissure remains in the body politic of Punjab based on communities rather than economic policies.

The fissures have sometimes erupted into violent instances as the minority Hindu community safeguards itself from marginalisation by leveraging its links and empathy with the larger Indian State or the Delhi Darbar as a metaphor. These fissures were originally engineered by the communal representation system introduced during colonial period. However, their continuity even a hundred years on is a failure of politics of Punjab and its political parties.

When Darbar Sahib gains extra territorial status, it will immediately excise the politics of 'threat to Sikh Qaum and GurSikhi' from Punjab's politics. It will give an opportunity for Punjab's politics to focus on issues that matter such as development, investment, welfare, education, etc. Political parties will have to focus on these and show results during their tenure as Government rather than conceal their failures by appealing to communalised political issues.

Punjab has the potential to be a major economic powerhouse of the region. It has to free itself from the divisive politics that were introduced during colonialism, that led to the death of nearly a million Punjabis in 1947 and that continue to dominate its political agendas, its security situation and its developmental issues.

Extra territorial status will be beneficial to Punjab, to India and Sri Darbar Sahib as well as to Global Sikh community. It will evolve into one of the most constructive partnerships for the region.

ADVANTAGES TO INDIA

Punjab is a border State; a very dynamic state and it also has a significant Punjabi diaspora community around the world. A restless border state with recurrent internal challenges within the state and to the larger Indian State poses a security threat to India, particularly with a hostile neighbour, Pakistan. Since 1947, India has failed to address issues in Punjab or convince Sikhs that their belief system is not facing assimilation in India. Moreover, the unique socio-political system of Sikhs with the Akal Takht treated as a supreme authority by Sikhs, is often seen as a competing authority by the Indian State.

An arrangement whereby Sri Akal Takht Sahib has extra territorial status will persuade the Sikhs that GurSikhi is secure and Sikhs can exercise independence of decisions without being seen as challenging the constitutional sovereignty of India. The often used campaign slogan 'panth khatre mein' by the Akalis will lose currency and the state can be a properly integrated state without perpetual internal and sometimes violent struggles.

A border state has to be secure otherwise it remains a weak link in the border security. A border state that is focussed on internal insecurities rather than threats to the larger State does not bode well for the country's overall security. Moreover, it siphons large amount of resources both to deal with internal security, border security and cross border incursions. These resources could be better spent in development and building infrastructure rather than unnecessary security threats. This merely needs a political will to address it.

If India wins over the Sikhs, there is also significant windfall that India can enjoy. A large Punjabi Sikh diaspora community will want to be associated more robustly with Punjab and invest in India. Currently both are restrained because a significant section of the Sikh community is either engaged in a campaign for Khalistan (independent Sikh State) or continues to feel that issues remain between it and India that need resolving.

Sikhs continue to be a powerful group in the UK, Canada and USA. Harnessing that power will be a significant boost to India's soft power in the world.

ADVANTAGES TO SOUTH ASIA

The perpetual tensions between the two nuclear neighbours have sometimes left the world on tender hooks as the threat of a nuclear war appears imminent when conflict escalates. While Pakistan has tried to involve third parties, India has refused to entertain that idea. There is no independent place for both countries to meet except in international meetings such as at a UN forum, SAARC (South Asian Association for Regional Cooperation) or sidelines of ASEAN (Association of South East Asian Nations). But prerogatives of political rhetoric often make it impossible for the two parties to sit together.

A Sri Darbar Sahib which remains outside the jurisdiction of India offers an opportunity as an independent place for discreet and even open diplomacy to find solutions within the region among the main States in South Asia.

Further, the Sikh population has deep roots in both countries. It sees both as important to its history and its current emotional attachments to places of reverence since the Sikh Gurus have been engaged in significant events, activities and settling communities in both sides of the Punjab. Guru Nanak Dev Ji, the founder of Sikhi, was born in Nankana Sahib, which is in Pakistan.

With an extraterritorial arrangement, Sri Darbar Sahib will be an institution that will encourage Sikhs to work for peace between both countries as their own historical interests lie in both neighbours being peaceful partners in the region.

The unintended benefits to the region can be speculated but the peace dividend could be one of the most significant benefits of Sri Akal Takht Sahib establishing a self-governing status as an institution enjoying supremacy without any legal or political shadow over it.

SUMMARY

In summary, there is a need for Sikhs to be interactive in the international sphere both to contribute to it and to concentrate on the issues of Sikhs across the world. Secondly, the status of Sri Akal Takht Sahib coordinating the supremacy of Guru Granth-Guru Panth needs to be restored in real terms so that the Sikh philosophy could engage with the world from a position of some degree of independence and self-juristic platform. Thirdly the Sikhs need to go back to the concept of non-territorial globalised nationhood sustained through their own institutional system, which will help strengthen their commitments and bonds within the countries they live in. Fourthly, Punjab, India and even South Asia will benefit from an extra territorial arrangement for Sri Darbar Sahib.

These can be realised if the changed circumstances of the Sikh demography as one now spread around the world is recognised as well as the real politick of South Asia is acknowledged. The opportunities are there. The road map is evident. It needs political will and Waheguru's blessing.

JASDEV SINGH RAI

GLOSSARY

AAP

AAP stands for Aam Aadmi Party, a political party in India.

Akali Dal

Akali Dal is a shortened word for Shiromani Akali Dal.

Akhand Kirtani Jatha

This is a school of interpretation within Sikhs.

Amritdhari

Amritdhari is a Sikh who makes a deeper commitment to Sikhi and is initiated into the order of the Khalsa. An Amritdhari Sikh lives a life of discipline as ordained in the Rehat Maryada

Chief Khalsa Dewan

This is a body set up by Sikhs in 1902 to stave off the increasing missionary efforts of other religious orders to convert Sikhs into their religions. The Khalsa Dewan set up several schools, colleges, orphanages and coordinated a new reform of 'Sikhism'. It was seen as elitist.

Congress Party

The Congress Party is an old political party that led the movement for decolonisation and then was in power in India continuously from 1947 until 1977.

Dam Dami Taksal

This is one of the oldest Sikh seminaries.

Dharam

The beliefs and philosophical systems of India are called Dharam rather than religion. Dharam has a wide meaning and is difficult to translate. It refers to the natural order of everything, or the character, nature and reality of everything or a single thing, life form, etc. So, there is the dharam of a stone, of a cloud, of human society, of all of existence, of cosmos, etc.

Gurdwara Act 1925

The Gurdwara Act was introduced in 1925 under British Indian Government. Many historic Gurdwaras had come into individual ownership through sitting occupant property law under British colonialism. This was unacceptable to Sikhs, particularly as some of the Gurdwaras were being used by the legal owners as brothels, dancing venues, etc. After a lengthy five-year struggle by Sikhs, the Government relented and passed legislation to legally transfer ownership of Gurdwaras from individual occupier owners to the community. The Act also provided for a Board to manage all these historic shrines. The Board came to be known as SGPC.

GurSikh

A Gursikh is a person who follows the teachings of the Gurus.

Guru

Guru is a traditional concept in India. It refers to an enlightened person who guides individuals or teachers from the confusion and darkness of ordinary life to enlightenment.

Jathedar

Jathedar is traditionally the head of the Sarbat Khalsa. Originally Jathedars were chosen by consensus at every convention. Subsequently the Jathedar became an established guardian of the office of Sri Akal Takht Sahib to manage the institution of Sri Akal Takht Sahib, all decisions made by Sarbat Khalsa and mediate on issues of interpretations, political differences and social concerns.

Kirtan
Singing the stanzas of Guru Granth Sahib. The Guru Granth Sahib has mostly been compiled in Raagas. However, kirtan is not always performed in the raag. Singing other compilations around the immortal and Sikh beliefs is also called kirtan. Kirtan is mostly sung in Gurdwaras.

Paath
Recitation of Sri Guru Granth Sahib.

Rehat Maryada
Rehat Maryada is the Sikh code of conduct. The Rehat Maryada is a series of rules and expectations based on interpretation of Guru Granth Sahib. They are decided by highly knowledgeable Sikhs and then presented to the Sarbat Khalsa for final acceptance. The current Rehat Maryada was finalised in 1936. Some changes were introduced by the SGPC in 1945.

SGPC
SGPC is abbreviation of Shiromani Gurdwara Parbhandik Committee.

Shiromani Gurdwara Parbhandik Committee
Shiromani Gurdwara Parbhandik Committee is a statutory body that manages most Sikh shrines and Gurdwaras in Punjab, including Sri Darbar Sahib Complex. Initially it was formed in a large gathering of Sikhs on 15th November 1920. In 1925, the British Indian Government passed legislation to transfer historic shrines from individual ownership

to community ownership and management. This was the 1925 Gurdwara Act. The Act established a board which adopted the name Shiromani Gurdwara Parbhandik Committee. It has elected members. It is the most powerful organisation among the Sikhs.

Sri Akal Takht Sahib

Literally the 'Immortal Throne' or Throne of the Immortal. Built around 1608 by the sixth Sikh Guru, Guru Hargobind Sahib. It is the seat of interpretational authority, decisions on individual and group conduct, Sikh consensus and collective political expression.

Sri Darbar Sahib Complex

Sri Darbar Sahib Complex is the name for the whole complex that has Sri Harmandir Sahib, Sri Akal Takht Sahib and a few more historical institutions. Sometimes it is just referred to as Sri Darbar Sahib.

Sri Guru Granth Sahib

Sri Guru Granth Sahib is the living guru of the Sikhs in Shabad form, or in written form. The Guru Granth Sahib has been compiled by the Sikh Gurus and comprises their teachings. The compilation is in poetry and raags. The Tenth Guru passed on the Guruship to the Granth and hence the Ad Sri Granth became Guru Granth Sahib as a living guru. The word Guru means a living teacher who guides from darkness to enlightenment.

Sri Harmandir Sahib

Sri Harmandir Sahib is the most revered holy place of the Sikhs. The Sarovar (water tank) was started by the third Guru, Guru Amardas Ji. It continued to be built by the fourth Guru, Guru Ramdas Ji in 1557. The final architectural shape of the buildings including the Sarovar was designed, built and completed by the fifth guru, Guru Arjun

Dev Ji in 1601. The building was covered with gold leaf on the upper half by Maharaja Ranjit Singh in 1830. It started being referred to as the Golden Temple in English under British rule. The only routine in Sri Harmandir Sahib is readings of Sri Guru Granth Sahib and Kirtan from Sri Guru Granth Sahib. No speeches, discussions, sermons or other ceremonies are held. Almost every Sikh aspires to visit Sri Harmandir Sahib once in their lifetime. Sri Harmandir Sahib is also known as Sri Darbar Sahib.

Sarbat Khalsa

Convention of worldwide Amritdhari Sikhs to develop consensus and decide on important matters is known as Sarbat Khalsa. The Sarbat Khalsa started essentially as an assembly of different groups and individuals at least once a year at Diwali and sometimes twice a year. The Sarbat Khalsa has not taken place for a long time as the Sikhs are now spread across the world. Discussions are taking place on how to reconstitute the assembly.

Shiromani Akali Dal

Shiromani Akal Dali is a political party established by the Sikhs on 15th November 1920. It was set up to represent the Sikhs in the communal representation system in politics set up by the British. The party continued after 1947 and has dominated the politics of Punjab. It declared itself a secular party in 2008.

Qaum

The word Qaum is used for a nation or 'People'. The Sikhs use it as a term for the entire Sikh community.

ABOUT THE AUTHOR

Dr Jasdev Singh Rai, MBChB (Lvpool). MA politics (SOAS).

Jasdev works as an Otolaryngologist and is Director of Sikh Human Rights Group (SHRG) since 1989. The organisation has special consultative status with United Nations. He is visiting Clinical Professor on Human Rights at the American University of Sovereign Nations, Arizona. He is the General Secretary of the British Sikh Consultative Forum and Chair of Worldviews of Nature Project. He has led several SHRG teams at United Nations conferences around human rights, transnationals, environment and diversity.

Jasdev has been involved in Sikh issues since 1984 when Sri Darbar Sahib (Golden Temple) was attacked by the Indian State. After taking up issues of human rights violations, it became evident to Jasdev that the deeper issue was the tension between the Supremacy of Sri Akal Takht Sahib in the Global Sikh community or Qaum and the Sovereignty of the Indian State after 1947. While neither agreeing or disagreeing with the issue of a Sikh State, a demand that arose in 1945, Jasdev sees that as a separate matter from the essential conflict that arose in the 1984 attack and which brought the issue of lack of settlement to the fore.

Jasdev has championed Sikh values and civilisation in international forums. He has championed human rights of several communities and regions at the UN. He is actively campaigning for a UN Declaration on Diversity, promoting pluralism and plural approaches to Environmental and Climate Change issues. His work has led to changes in law in UK after the Chahal case. His work on human Rights also led to changes in policies and legal decisions in India. He has written and published academic papers on ethics, gender foeticide, anti terrorism, freedom of conscience, conflict resolution and Sikh philosophy. He has written three books including Universalism and Ethical Values of Environment for UNESCO and Anekantvada, Indian Pluralism.

Milton Keynes UK
Ingram Content Group UK Ltd.
UKHW040619111123
432387UK00002B/51